REFUGEE REALITIES

VOICES FROM THE MIDDLE EAST

TARA SEGER

WITH LESSON IDEAS FOR TEACHERS

To my sons, my nephew, and the youth of America:
May you always understand the importance of
your birthright as American citizens.
May you always remember that our perspectives
depend on our circumstances.
May you understand, and empathize with,
the struggles of the individuals of the globe.

For My Father: For always inspiring me
to pursue my passions.

"Please, if you see a refugee, or any type of different person, try to be nice to them. Believe me, you might save a life or a future. Because sometimes, I lose hope entirely. But then a small gesture by a stranger, a neighbor, or anyone can change my day and my thoughts. We are people like you. We have dreams and hopes; we just need a chance in life. You can make a difference, so please try to."

—Layla, Syrian refugee presently residing in Istanbul, Turkey

CONTENTS

PREFACE

It has been an absolute honor to interview the refugees highlighted in this book. Most people cannot imagine what it would truly feel like to lose not only your home, but your ability to live in your country. What would it feel like to be forced to give up everything you know and move to an entirely new setting? What items would you bring with you? Would you be able to find work? Where would you live? Who would help you? What family members would make the journey alongside you? Would you be homesick? What, or who, would you long for the most?

Deciding to uproot your life and make an arduous journey to another country is certainly a life altering and heart breaking decision. What are the push factors that make refugees decide to attempt this feat? I decided to reach out to my connections around the world, and to retain a grant from the *Qatar Foundation*, to interview refugees and prepare their stories for young minds to read in a digestible fashion.

Rahim from Iraq was my initial inspiration. The tragic stories of his young life in Iraq, his refuge in Iran, and his struggles with his ultimate move to Europe, are absolutely fascinating. He spent hours revealing to me his unimaginable challenges. His smile revealed an appreciation that I empathized with what he went through and that I wanted his story to be shared.

Layla from Syria is a young mom. She wants what's best for her children. After years of risking bodily harm to protest against Bashar al Assad's regime she decided that fleeing to Turkey was best. She and I bonded easily. Her passion for revealing to the world the reality of living under Bashar al Assad's regime inspired me even more to get this book published and to get her message to the world.

Balsam is an Ezidi (Yezidi) who fled Sinjar two hours before it was overrun by ISIS. He revealed to me the nightmare of the genocide of his town as pragmatically as possible. I did my best to hold back tears as he poured out a story that no one should have to tell. His ability to move on from that tragedy and focus on offering his family a happy life in France is a tribute to his spirit and courage.

Salam from Yemen is young and sweet. She did much research by collaborating with her friends to make sure every detail of the story of the Yemeni people was revealed. Her spirit and energy shine through; but she also reveals deep seated fear for her friends and family still living in a war zone.

Orit from Israel has spent hours speaking with my American students. She visits my classes eager to reveal the story of Israel with an extensive google slideshow of past histories and current events. Her dedication to her country is steadfast. Her bravery as a navy soldier is truly admirable. She always has a positive attitude, even when air raid sirens went off on her sister's wedding day. Her courage amazes me.

Salman from the West Bank is relatable and easy to talk to. The students are always inspired by his vastly different thoughts about the Palestinian and Israeli conflict when compared to my Israeli guest speakers. He has explained to me the Palestinian perspective in a completely unique and relatable fashion. Salman also requested the opportunity to speak to one of my Jewish contacts from Israel- as he has an open mind- and he never met anyone from the other side of the wall before. The three of us held a worthwhile conversation together on zoom. It ended on friendly terms and we all still contact one another occasionally on Whatsapp to discuss our thoughts on the headlines.

Joanna has a vibrant personality. Her ultimate goal is to be a good mother. When she reveals the economic struggles she endures in Lebanon I become intensely frustrated for her family and her whole country.

Malika and Mohammad from Afghanistan were my last interview. I decided to focus on Afghanistan last to give recent arrivals who witnessed the American withdrawal of 2022 an opportunity to settle into the United States before I requested an emotional interview with them. This interview had its own unique challenge. Malika spoke no English and Mohammad translated everything for her. Since I have been working with refugees for years, I realized that I had become quite skilled in understanding English from a variety of accents. When I met this sweet couple I never dreamed that this small, cordial woman was a member of the Afghan Special Forces and had engaged in over 500 missions against the Taliban in support of the coalition forces.

All of the refugees interviewed in this book have amazing abilities to overcome challenges. They are all truly inspiring.

It has been my pleasure to reveal human stories from conflict zones in the Middle East. As an educator for almost 20 years, I have determined one critical truth: students need to understand the human story in order to fully understand history and current events.

The purpose of this book is to create a connection that bonds us in order to inspire international camaraderie. This can begin when the human story is revealed and we start to understand the challenging circumstances that individuals from Middle Eastern nations face. Please take the time to familiarize yourself with the struggles of the human beings in this book who poured their hearts out to reveal their personal stories to you.

It is critical that students understand the truth of what is happening around the globe. As an educator, I've made it a priority to emphasize current events. I designed my own course entitled *"Current Middle East Conflicts"*. An entire school year with high school juniors and seniors is devoted to focusing on what is happening in the Middle East and the recent history that led to these situations. One of the most important elements of making this course a success is the many Middle Eastern contacts I have made over the years. I reach out to my contacts all over the world to get their unique perspectives on the situations happening around them.

I have done extensive research and professional development focused on the Middle East. For example, I was selected to participate in a Teacher Study Tour of the United Arab Emirates with the World Affairs Council. Additionally, I presented my unique *"Current Middle East Conflicts"* curriculum at the SOCIOINT International Education Conference on Social Studies and Humanities in Istanbul, Turkey in 2019. I was also selected for the 2022 Advanced Learning Program at Yad Vashem, the world-renowned Holocaust museum in Jerusalem, Israel.

The refugee stories in this book are presented in an easy-to-read fashion. My goal is for teachers to be able to use these stories in their classrooms to expose students to the human element involved in conflict zones. This book may be used for the personal development of adults or adolescents, or by teachers in a classroom setting. Each story is designed with a teacher-friendly model in mind. Sections of each person's personal story are broken down to make it easier for students to comprehend. Guiding questions are suggested for brainstorming and reflection. Also included is a list of necessary vocabulary to enhance student understanding and engagement. It is suggested that anyone reading the book reviews the vocabulary first, then takes a few moments to reflect on the guiding question(s). Teachers may use the guiding questions to facilitate pre-reading discussions with students. At the end of each section the guiding questions are referred back to. Please take a moment to reflect on the guiding questions listed at the end of each section whether you are reading alone or with a group of students. Taking the opportunity to stop and reflect on what has been read allows the brain to digest the material, fully retaining it before moving on. This reflection opportunity also prevents the reader from becoming overwhelmed with content and offers a chance for the reader to stop and empathize with each story.

Years ago, I decided that it is not enough to simply expose students to the realities faced by people in war zones through photos, readings, videos and discussions. Students need to have a real interaction with someone who is actually affected by the conflict in order to fully empathize with the dire conditions. This is why I thoroughly enjoy working with *Natakallam*. This organization connects teachers and students with refugees from all over the world. *Natakallam* hires refugees to act as "conversation partners" with students. They teach foreign languages, discuss cultural traditions of people from countries all over the world, and/or discuss current events with students throughout the US via zoom. At the end of all of my units covering conflict zones, I always reach out to *NaTakallam* for a real conversation with a refugee from the area the students studied. I cannot thank *NaTakallam* enough for connecting me and my students with conversation partners. They all have relatable personalities and truly engage young minds.

This is the link to the *NaTakallam* website:
https://natakallam.com/education/

The purchase of this book comes with a 15% off coupon code for a conversation with a refugee through *NaTakallam*. The coupon code is listed at the end of the book in the Acknowledgments section. Teachers are more than welcome to share this code with their students as well.

Scholarships for conversations are also available through the *Qatar Foundation*.

The names of each participant in the book has been changed in an effort to protect their privacy and identities.

CHAPTER ONE

AN INTERVIEW WITH BALSAM
AN EZIDI* REFUGEE WHO ESCAPED ISIS IN IRAQ

O n August 7, 2014, Vian Dakhil, a female, and the only Ezidi member of Iraq's parliament, fought back tears and a shaking voice as she begged the Iraqi Parliament to save her people from genocide. ISIS (The Islamic State of Iraq and Syria) was attempting to exterminate the Ezidi people. She stated that the Ezidis:

> "are being slaughtered under the banner of 'there is no God but Allah'. Mr. Speaker, until now 500 Ezidi men have been slaughtered.... Women are being taken as slaves and sold in the slave market.... Please, brothers... there is now a campaign of genocide being waged on the Ezidi constituent.... Brothers, away from all political disputes, we want humanitarian solidarity. I speak here in the name of humanity, save us! Save us!"

---

*   Ezidi is often translated as Yezidi.

She continued.

> *"For 48 hours, 30,000 families are besieged in the Sinjar mountain without water and food. They are dying. 70 babies have died so far from thirst and suffocation. 50 old people have died from deteriorating conditions. Our women are taken as slaves and sold in the slave market.... We are being slaughtered. We are being exterminated. An entire religion is being exterminated from the face of the Earth. Brothers, I appeal to you in the name of humanity to save us!"*

ISIS led a campaign to exterminate the Ezidi people in 2014. Men were murdered, and ISIS engaged in unspeakable torture of the women they kidnapped and often sold for profit. There are countless stories of the brutality of ISIS. One such disturbing story is that of an Ezidi woman who was kidnapped with her child. They were held separately. She was starved for several days. Finally, her ISIS captor brought her a plate of food with rice and some meat. She ate the food on her plate. She was told afterwards that the meat was her own child (https://says.com/my/news/an-iraqi-lawmaker-claims-isis-tricked-a-mother-into-eating-her-own-son).

But how was ISIS, a terrorist organization infamous for its brutality, able to become powerful enough to nearly exterminate an entire religion?

To understand this, historians refer back to 2001. The September 11th attacks horrified the American people. Osama bin Laden planned the attacks from Afghanistan; 15 of the hijackers were from Saudi Arabia, two were from the UAE, one was from Lebanon and one was from Egypt. Despite these facts, the

---

*   https://www.wbur.org

United States was suffering from a severe case of Islam-ophobia that was aimed at all Muslims and Muslim nations.

The US had already engaged in a brief war with Iraq, a Muslim nation, in 1991 over its invasion of Kuwait. By 2001, the American people still feared this Muslim country and the US government had a strained relationship with Iraq's president, Saddam Hussein. Since the withdrawal in 1991, Iraq was under severe sanctions due to fears that President Hussein may have nuclear facilities enriching enough uranium for a nuclear weapon. Hussein chose to let his country spiral into economic depravity from the sanctions rather than meet UN requirements to disarm. The United States government was afraid that Hussein had weapons of mass destruction that could be used in a surprise attack on US soil, one that could possibly be worse than the Sept. 11th attacks.

War fervor grew and the American public widely supported another invasion of Iraq in 2003.

President Sadaam Hussein of Iraq and his Baathist Party were Sunni Muslims. Sunni and Shia Muslims have historically been at odds with each other since the death of the Prophet Muhammad and the original disagreement over who should be the next caliph, or religious leader of Islam, following the Prophet Muhammad.

When the Sunni Baathist party was in power in Iraq under Saddam Hussein from 1979 until 2003, the party made every effort to subjugate the Shia majority in Iraq. In 2003, the American coalition, under George W. Bush, removed Saddam Hussein and the Baathist Party from control in Iraq. Nouri al-Maliki was propped up as the deputy leader of the Supreme National De-Baathification Commission of the Iraqi interim government. What Iraq truly needed was a government that would unite the Sunni, Shia, Kurd, and Ezidi. Unfortunately, the new Shia government returned the treatment they had received from the Sunni, and began subjugating them. Eventually, many of these newly subjugated Sunni joined ISIS as a form of revenge against the Shia.

Under the Obama administration, the American troops withdrew from Iraq in December of 2011. The mostly Shia Iraqi forces, trained by the US military, were not equipped enough to effectively protect a country without American support. By 2014, much of Iraq rapidly fell into the hands of ISIS including Baghdad, Mosul, Fallujah, and Hit.

By 2014, ISIS was strong enough to invade the Sinjar mountain villages and attempt to completely eradicate all Ezidi people from the face of the earth. They were convinced the Ezidi people were devil worshipers and needed to be murdered in support of Allah.

BALSAM'S STORY

Balsam grew up in the Ezidi community of Sinjar. He classified Sinjar as unified community. As a child, he and his friends spent hours entertaining themselves in the backyard. They usually played soccer while the girls played with dolls inside the homes.

As a child, Balsam grew up with no father between the ages of 3 and 13. Iraq was at war with Iran from Sept. of 1980 until Aug. of 1988. His father became a prisoner of war in Iran for ten years. He was taken prisoner in 1980 and returned in 1990. The only communication he had with his father was through letters. They exchanged photographs of each other two or three times per year. His father wrote recommendations for him and his siblings from prison such as obey your grandfather and be kind to your mother.

When his father returned he was inspired by how happy his

grandfather and his uncle were to have his father home. It took about two or three years for him and his siblings to fully adjust to their father's return. They were accustomed to treating their grandfather as their father. The more Balsam grew, the closer his relationship became with his father.

As an adult, Balsam decided to marry and have a family of his own. He was determined to give his four children a better life than he had and a relationship with a father who was always present and supportive in their lives. He worked as a teacher and as a translator for coalition forces during the second Iraq War.

Balsam and his wife and four children fled Sinjar two hours before it was overrun by ISIS. They barely escaped with their lives. Today they live safely in France, but they have many terrible memories and worry for the safety of their friends and family that remain in Iraq.

PART ONE

Ezidi: (Yezidi) A monotheistic religion that also believes that the world was entrusted to the care of seven angels. Each angel was assigned different tasks by God. The chief angel is Tawos-malik; he is responsible for the rest of the angels. Ezidis also believe that there is a hell, Satan exists, and that there are evil souls.

Sinjar: A town in northern Iraq. It is five kilometers south of the Sinjar mountains. Primarily, Ezidis live in Sinjar.

Satan: The evil entity that Jews, Christians, Ezidis, and Muslims believe encourages humans to sin.

Prophet: "A person regarded as an inspired teacher or proclaimer of the will of God" (Oxford Languages).

Visa: "An endorsement on a passport that allows the holder to enter another country" (resources.evoyglobal.com).

GUIDING QUESTION

How can rumors be destructive?

I interviewed Balsam on December 4, 2021. We met via zoom. He was in France. I was in the United States.

Balsam has a welcoming expression and he does his best to be cheerful despite the horrific and unsettling tales he tells. His expression reveals a sadness that is hidden behind his gentle demeanor.

One of the first questions I asked him was "were the Ezidis discriminated against throughout your entire life?"

"Yes, we were. I always knew that my religion was different from all of the other religions in my country, Iraq. Whenever we left the Sinjar area, people would point at us and say those people are Ezidis. We never understood why they treated us badly just because we are Ezidis, or why being something different meant that we were something bad in the community."

"How did they know that you were different? Did you dress differently?" I asked.

"Yes, we dress differently. We talk differently. We speak a different dialect. There are certain things that we don't purchase at stores. One example is lettuce. This is because in 1246 the Ezidi leader Sheikh Hassan bin Adi was killed by the Emir of Mosul during one of the genocides against the Ezidi people. According to my oral family tradition, the Muslims of Mosul watered the lettuce fields with the blood of 80,000 Ezidi people. So when we go to stores we stay away from the lettuce. People sometimes noticed if we didn't buy lettuce and often they asked us questions. They might ask, where are you from, or are you Muslim or Ezidi or Christian?

Also, until the late 1990s, the Ezidi people never wore the color blue. The men dressed in white and the women dressed very differently from the other women of other communities. The Ezidis refrain from wearing the color blue because of the beauty of the blue sky. We believe the color blue is only for heaven, not for human beings.

Another Ezidi tradition is that when the Prophet Muhammad died the Muslims wore the color blue to signify that they were in mourning. This color blue became associated with sadness because of the death of the Prophet Muhammad; so we don't wear it.

The Ezidis also traditionally grow mustaches. Some of

these things are what made us recognizable to people of other religions.

There is also a rumor that the Ezidi people worship the devil. During the Ottoman Era, claiming that the Ezidi people worship the devil was an excuse to commit genocide against us. Traditionally, we believe that there is a chief angel that is closest to God. The Christians and Muslims believe that Satan was the strongest archangel and that he fell from grace because he refused to bow to Adam. The Ezidi worship of the chief angel spurred the rumor that Ezidis worship Satan by wrongfully equating our chief angel with Satan.

According to Ezidi tradition, Tawosmalik also translated Tawuse Malak, is the chief angel. He is the nearest angel to God. When God created the world he ordered that the angels never obey any other being. When God created Adam, the first human, God asked the seven angels to pray to Adam. All seven angels knelt down, other than Tawosmalik, who said that you ordered us not to kneel to anything other than you God. For doing this, Tawosmalik was actually rewarded with the sacred angel circle because he passed God's test. Ezidis believe that God was testing the angels to make sure that they would never kneel for anyone other than God. This is why Ezidi people always wear shirts that have a circular collar; it represents the sacred circle that was given to Tawosmalik for passing the test.

We do worship Tawosmalik, our chief angel. We also believe in Satan as a different entity and we do not worship him.

Most of the genocide against Ezidis occurred during the Ottoman Era under the false pretense that the Ezidis worship the devil. But the discrimination never fully went away. It ebbed and flowed.

For example, in the 1970's, my parents had to leave their hometown in Iraq because the government made them move from their mountain neighborhood and settle in the desert.

This was done so that the government could easily control them. The Ezidi people lost their visas. They had minimal access to water, electricity, transportation, and medical services. The government took all services from them in order to control them. We also used to be free from joining the military when we lived in the mountainous communities because the government couldn't control us and conscript us into the military. This was another example of how we were discriminated against over the false accusation that our worship of our chief angel means that we worship the devil."

GUIDING QUESTION

How did a rumor destroy the reputation of the Ezidis?

PART TWO

VOCAB

Propaganda: "Persuasive mass communication that filters and frames the issues of the day in a way that strongly favours particular interests" (oxfordreference.com).

Minority community: "A group of people whose practices, race, religion, ethnicity, or other characteristics are fewer in numbers than the main groups of those classifications" (Wikipedia).

Mosque: A religious place of worship for Muslim people.

Imam: A Muslim leader of prayer.

GUIDING QUESTIONS

Why is it important to understand the difference between fact and propaganda? What is the importance of always making up your own mind?

"Do you have any idea why ISIS thought it was necessary to destroy Ezidi statues in museums?" I asked.

"Whenever a criminal commits a crime, they try to leave no trace of the crime behind. What ISIS did was an attempt to completely erase the entire memory of the Ezidi people from the face of the Earth. They wanted no witnesses behind to tell the story of the massacre of the Ezidi people. So they decided not only to destroy the people, but also to destroy their history. ISIS thought that if they could erase the Ezidi people's history then they could erase their identity as well.

The destruction of our statues was scary but it wasn't what made me decide to leave Iraq. My children are what made me decide to leave Iraq. I wanted my children to live somewhere safe.

In 1996, I was living in a Muslim community in Iraq to attend a university. During Friday prayers there is always a speech from the imam. It is public and everyone can hear it. I could overhear the speeches from the imams every Friday. They called for discrimination against minority groups, including the Ezidi people. They stated essentially that the Muslim community is the best and they very aggressively talked poorly of the minority communities.

I also had a Muslim friend that warned me that it is dangerous for me to stay in Iraq. My friend said to me 'if you ever have a chance to get out of Iraq, do it because they are going to kill you. Do you know what they are saying? They are praying that whatever the Ezidi people own, including property, children and women, will one day become their property.'

We don't know what else was happening at the mosques but people were meeting there regularly. Sometimes people were going to the mosque seven times per day. This seems like a very nice thing to do. It is nice to go and pray seven times a day; that is good. But we didn't know what else was going on behind the mosque doors.

In the streets, we saw normal people, neighbors who lived nearby, starting to believe that they were better than us. We believed that this mindset came from the mosque."

GUIDING QUESTION

What form of propaganda was used to stir hate of the Ezidi people? If Iraqi children were more educated regarding forms of propaganda might the massacre of the Ezidis have been avoided or less widespread?

PART THREE

VOCAB

Crimes Against Humanity: "Specific crimes committed in the control of a large-scale attack targeting civilians, regardless of their nationality. These crimes include murder, torture, sexual violence, enslavement, persecution, enforced disappearance, etc." (trialinternational.org).

NGO: (Non-governmental organization) "A nonprofit organization that operates independently of any government, typically one whose purpose is to address a social or political issue" (Oxford Languages).

GUIDING QUESTION

Why is it important to push back against discrimination when we see it?

"How did you know to leave Sinjar before ISIS attacked your village?" I asked.

"I didn't know for certain that we were about to be attacked. But I did know that all of the areas surrounding Sinjar had been taken by ISIS. I knew that things were becoming very dangerous. I happened to leave the very morning that ISIS attacked my village; I left two hours before ISIS invaded my neighborhood. I had no idea where to go with my wife and four daughters. We had no food, water, or visas.

My ten-year-old daughter kept asking me questions. She wanted to know why we were leaving and why we were packing up all of our things. She wanted to know why I was worried and why everyone was leaving Sinjar. We told her that we needed to leave the house for a few days, but that we would return.

We just got in the car and left home. We considered going to the top of the mountain in Sinjar, or to the Syrian border, or to the northern portion of Iraq. There was no plan. ISIS took over all of the territory surrounding Sinjar in only two months; we had no time to prepare an escape.

There were men in my village who volunteered to stay and fight ISIS so that the women and children could try to escape to the mountains. They managed to stall ISIS somewhat. The Peshmerga force (PKK) was supposed to defend the Sinjar area. It was frustrating because most of them fled out of fear of ISIS. However, some of them stayed.

When ISIS started attacking the southern villages of Sinjar the remaining Peshmerga forces knew they would not be able to hold ISIS back. They recommended that all of the Ezidis in the northern Sinjar villages leave their homes and head to the top of the mountain for their safety. They were told to bring food and to wait it out before they returned. My family and I were lucky that our homes were in the northern parts of Sinjar because the clashes started in the southern parts of Sinjar. Because I lived in the north, I had a bit more time to escape compared to the unfortunate ones who lived to the south of Sinjar.

The clashes in Sinjar villages began on Aug. 2, 2014 at 10:00 AM. They continued until August 3, 2014 at 8:00 AM. By this time, most of the Ezidi men were murdered and the remaining men had no weapons. Thanks to the bravery of the men who stayed behind to fight, 90% of the Ezidi people were able to escape with their lives.

Everyone who decided to stay behind, thinking that they would not be murdered, unfortunately were very wrong. They were all killed or sold into slavery. We did not expect the violence to reach the level of cruelty that it reached. It was extremely severe, especially for the women and children. We expected that they would kill all of the men. That was a somewhat anticipated idea because the Ezidis endured genocide several times throughout history. Psychologically we were prepared for the murder of the men; but we didn't expect to lose everything, even the women and the children.

It was very sad to see neighbors that we recognized from Iraq join ISIS and attempt to slaughter everyone in our neighborhoods. Our own Arab neighbors joined ISIS and gave them important information about our whereabouts. They also stole our belongings and sold them for a profit, or kept them for themselves. When the PKK returned, and took our village back over, they found our belongings inside the homes of our Arab neighbors.

My home was used by ISIS as a kitchen. It was destroyed by missiles dropped by the coalition forces against ISIS.

There are many terrible stories about what happened to the Ezidi women. One such story is about a young girl who was my neighbor. She was taken by an emir of ISIS. She recognized one of the ISIS soldiers under her kidnapper's command. She ran to him for help because he was a friend of her father's. He had visited her home frequently as a guest. She was very surprised when the soldier informed her that he only pretended to be her father's friend because he found her attractive and he had planned on kidnapping her all along.

After she endured much torture, her family did manage to gather together funds to purchase their daughter back. When she returned, she told her family about the man who pretended to be her father's friend. They were shocked that he acted as a family friend but had evil intentions all along.

Unfortunately, similar stories are common. Ezidi people often welcomed Arabs into their homes as friends. We went to each other's parties, celebrations, and funerals. For years, Ezidis and Arabs were very close friends. They often became what we refer to as Blood Brothers. This is a tradition when a young boy is circumcised in the lap of an Arab. This Arab becomes a Blood Brother to the family. This is a tradition solidifying that Ezidi families and Arab families have become close friends. These same Arabs, who we thought were our Blood Brothers, stabbed us in the back by joining and assisting ISIS when they murdered our men and kidnapped, sold, and raped our women.

Luckily, my family escaped Sinjar two hours before ISIS overran my village. We decided against taking refuge in the mountains as the PKK recommended and headed towards Syria. This was the right decision because the people who headed for the mountains were stuck there living outdoors, exposed to the elements, with limited amounts of food for almost an entire month. Many of the children starved to death.

Upon our departure, there was a very long line of traffic because there were so many people trying to flee for their lives. People who had an extra truck or a car gave it to their neighbors so that their neighbors could try to escape ISIS' path of destruction.

While I was driving out of the village I saw my cousin, his wife, and their one and two year old babies. They had no vehicle. We decided to pack them into our four person Hyundai as well. My family is already six people. My children were ten, eight, five and four years old. With my cousin's family, we became ten people in a small car trying to drive away from ISIS.

The children were scared. They could tell that we were very worried; but they did not understand the gravity of the situation. Along the route we took on the highway we could see bullets and hear gunfire. In the neighborhoods nearby there were several Arab villages that welcomed the arrival of ISIS. While we were driving we could hear shooting happening in these villages. ISIS used PKC Russian style weapons. These weapons are very loud and have a distinct sound. We could visibly see bullets hitting the hills on the side of the road we were driving on. Some of the people who were stuck in the traffic behind us were shot to death while trying to drive away. We were absolutely terrified of what we could see and hear happening to the sides and behind us while we were stuck in traffic. We are lucky that we made it out alive.

The roadway to the Kurdish area in the north of Iraq was blocked. Instead, we decided to head towards Syria. My father-in-law gave me directions over the phone, guiding us towards Syria. While doing so, he received word that the border to the Kurdish area of Iraq was reopened. We headed there instead, though we feared for our lives because ISIS was strong and the Kurdish Peshmerga would have trouble protecting us if ISIS arrived there. We drove through the town of Rabia'a, the town that separates Sinjar from Kurdistan. This would usually be an hour and a half drive. The mass migration of Ezidi people trying to travel there caused so much traffic that it took us four hours to get there.

When we arrived in Kurdistan it was dark. We didn't know what to do or where to go. There were Kurdish people outside handing out sandwiches and water. It made us feel good that someone was giving us something to eat and drink; but we were still very nervous. We asked if ISIS had arrived in Kurdistan yet. They hadn't.

The Kurdish people told us to take shelter in the schools. There were also many Kurdish people who took in one or two Ezidi families for a night or two. The first night we arrived there we slept in a school classroom. We couldn't find a vacant hotel. All of the rooms were taken and we were exhausted. Aside from the sandwiches we received when we arrived, we hadn't eaten all day. The women and children, especially, were very afraid that ISIS would come and kill us. The terrible stories of the things that happened to the people who stayed at their homes were making their way to Kurdistan.

I managed to get to a store to find something to eat. I found a watermelon and brought it back to the school for my family. By the time I returned with the watermelon the children were already sleeping.

The next day I received a call from my brother. He told me that there was an unfinished building that my family could stay in temporarily. Even though the building was unfinished, it was like a palace. I had somewhere for my family to live.

It was challenging to live there because there was no running water or electricity. Also, there were two other families living there with us. There was no privacy because the walls and doors were not finished. Also, there were no windows and the home became extremely hot. We stayed there for one month.

At the end of the month, we found out that ISIS was about to invade Kurdistan. We decided to try to flee for Turkey. My two brothers and my uncle and I offered our cars to the smugglers as a form of trade to try to get them to smuggle us into Turkey. They refused to take our cars and demanded money instead. We didn't have enough so they refused to help us. We couldn't get across legally because we didn't have passports, but we couldn't stay because we would be murdered. We were desperate and terrified.

The next day the American air raids started. The air raids stopped ISIS' progress and saved Kurdistan, and quite possibly the lives of my family. This was the first time that we felt a sigh of relief.

I managed to rent a small basement apartment in Kurdistan for one month for my family. Then we started to run out of money so we had to return to the unfinished building. We lived there for two months. Many humanitarian organizations came to assist the Ezidi people when ISIS started withdrawing. I was hired as a data manager for the local NGOs and then I was able to rent a flat for my family.

I managed to work with a French NGO in the area. Eventually, they helped me get to the French Embassy in Iraq. I applied for a visa to move with my family to France and it was approved."

GUIDING QUESTION

How did the acceptance of the discrimination of the Ezidi people in Iraq ultimately lead to crimes against humanity?

PART FOUR

VOCAB
Sanction: "An action that is taken, or an order that is given, to force a country to obey international laws by limiting or stopping trade with that country, by not allowing economic aid for that country, etc" (MerriamWebster.com).

GUIDING QUESTION
How can pride get in the way of doing what is right?

"Balsam, what could have been done differently to prevent the genocide of the Ezidi people?" I asked.

"The UN could have done more to help. If only the Iraqi borders were protected, none of this would've happened. The Iraq border was open to five countries including the ones that were interfering in the politics of Iraq. The countries are Syria, Turkey, Iran, Kuwait, and Saudi Arabia. The United Nations could have controlled the border of Iraq the way that it was controlled by the United States in 2003. Controlling the border would have prevented the genocide, in particular, most ISIS members came through the borders of Turkey and Syria.

There are other problems that ultimately led to the recent genocide. The sanctions on Iraq caused a lot of animosity between groups of people such as the Sunni and the Shia. For example, as a young teen growing up in Iraq in the 1990s, before the US invasion of 2003, I had no money and I had to work eight hours per day to be paid only $2.50 per week. This equated to about 2,500 Iraqi dinars. It was never enough to eat well or have decent clothes to wear because there was always a shortage of goods and services due to the sanctions on

Iraq. My country was under severe sanctions from the United Nations because Saddam Hussein would not meet all requirements to disarm his weapons of mass destruction. That caused much economic devastation for people throughout Iraq. The Sunni felt less of the economic burden than the Shia and Ezidi endured, but they felt it as well.

I personally believe that Saddam Hussein would have used his weapons of mass destruction if he actually had them. So he let his people starve under the sanctions, and he allowed the economy to completely deteriorate, all because he had too much pride.

It was very promising when the US invaded Iraq and controlled the borders in 2003. When the US first invaded the economy picked up. There was hope that life would be better under American control. We thought the US would bring democracy, freedom, and happiness.

During the American invasion of 2003 I was working as a teacher. I was paid three dollars for one month of teaching. After the invasion, after one month of fighting and Saddam Hussein's execution and removal from power, I was instantly being paid $60 per month to teach. That was a big change and it helped me and my family to live in a better way. Unfortunately, when the US left Iraq in 2011, the economy crumbled and its border was left open. The Sunni were angry that Saddam Hussein, a Sunni, was hanged and the Shia were now controlling the government. This eventually caused the rise of ISIS and the genocide of the Ezidi people."

GUIDING QUESTION

How did Saddam Hussein let his pride get in the way of doing what was best for his country?

PART FIVE

VOCAB

PKK: "A militant Kurdish nationalist organization founded by Abdullah ("Apo") Öcalan in the late 1970s. Although the group initially espoused demands for the establishment of an independent Kurdish state, its stated aims were later tempered to calls for greater Kurdish autonomy" from Turkey, Iraq and Syria. (Britannica).

GUIDING QUESTION

Under what circumstances should a person give up their homeland and move somewhere new?

How did President Obama's withdrawal from Iraq in 2011 affect the situation in Iraq for the Ezidis?", I asked.

"One of the big mistakes that happened in 2010 was the deal between the Iraqi ex Prime Minister Maliki and President Obama to limit the number of US troops in Iraq. The US handed American military bases over to Iraqi troops. These troops were not well trained and it was useless to give them these military bases because ISIS was able to take them over easily. Iraq still needed security from the American troops, instead ISIS stole American military equipment from Iraqi troops.

The Iraqi soldiers themselves, who were supposed to man the checkpoints to protect the people in the different villages, were too afraid to stand guard at the checkpoints. They often ran and hid when cars came near the checkpoints. Iraqi generals didn't know what to do about this. Since Obama withdrew before the Iraqi soldiers were fully trained, ISIS was able to take over swaths of land and murder innocent people.

Unfortunately, ISIS is an ideology that will never go away. ISIS will do more terrorist attacks again. Today's date is December 4, 2021. It is still not safe for Ezidis to return to Sinjar because many armed groups are controlling the area. There is no central government controlling Sinjar. Right now, anyone in the Sinjar area could easily be a victim of clashes, robbery, or murder and these crimes would most likely go unpunished.

Who is controlling which town is always changing and you don't know what regions are safe and which ones are not. It is dangerous for anyone right now in Sinjar; but it is especially unsafe for the Ezidi people.

Even though ISIS is gone, Ezidis don't feel safe from our neighbors because they sided with ISIS, and against us, during the genocide. We are living in a tribal system in that area. Everyone knows everyone in Sinjar. All of the Ezidis know all of the Arabs and vice versa. We know what people were welcoming to ISIS and what people were not. We know who hurt our women and children and we know who didn't. We know that many of the culprits are now still freely living in the Sinjar region and there is no accountability for their criminal actions.

All of our neighbors have gotten away with their crimes. I have heard of only one case of an ISIS member who is actually being tried for the rape of an Ezidi girl.

The Iraqi government has not done a sufficient job of hunting down members of ISIS and putting them in prison. In fact, I have heard stories of the Iraqi government putting people of different political opinions into prison in Iraq under the false claim that they were members of ISIS, even though they were not. Therefore, we cannot trust the Iraq government when it comes to any figure regarding how many members of ISIS are in prison in Iraq.

When I go on social media, I see hundreds of photos of ISIS members, dressed in ISIS uniforms, accompanied by the stories of the horrific illegal acts they performed, uploaded by witnesses. All of these men have not been prosecuted and are still walking freely in Iraq.

There are also many armed groups there that came from Turkey and Syria, especially the PKK party, which is Kurdish. They are a target of Turkey. The Turks regard the Kurdish PKK party as a terrorist group. As of Dec of 2021, Turkey continues air raids against the PKK into Sinjar on a weekly basis. These raids often kill innocent Ezidi people.

The PKK was actually the only armed group that helped some of the Ezidis flee from the ISIS attacks in Sinjar. But now the PKK is taking over the area for themselves as opposed to saving the area for us.

There is no way to reconcile what happened to the Ezidi people. You can't teach that violence is wrong with more violence. The severity of what the Ezidi people endured is so severe that there is no proper punishment ISIS members could ever receive for what they did.

GUIDING QUESTION

Considering the circumstances, should Ezidis return home and reclaim their villages or move away?

PART SIX

GUIDING QUESTION
Why is it important to understand other people's perspectives?

"What should become of the orphaned Ezidi children who were fathered by ISIS?" I asked.

The Ezidi people decided to break cultural norms and accept the return of the women who have been sexually assaulted by ISIS. However, we cannot accept the children of ISIS members, even if they have Ezidi mothers. We feel terrible for the children. But for hundreds of years Ezidi people have endured torment and sacrifice to keep the Ezidi religion alive, including surviving many genocides. The Ezidi people believe that if they accept Muslim children into their community it will be an infiltration of the Ezidi community and it will mean the end of the Ezidis.

Some children who have Ezidi mothers and ISIS fathers remain in orphanages because their mothers have returned home. The children are not welcome into Ezidi villages. On the other hand, many orphaned Ezidi children remain in orphanages. Other Ezidi orphans live in Ezidi villages, being raised by aunts, uncles and cousins, because their parents were murdered by ISIS or are still missing.

A friend of mine who grew up down the street from me tried to purchase his sister back from an ISIS soldier, but he would not purchase her two children that were fathered by the ISIS soldier. His sister refused to return home without her children. Unfortunately, we do not hear any news from her anymore. We don't know if she lives with the ISIS fighter or if she lives somewhere on her own with the two children, or if she is even alive at all. We feel terrible about this; but we were nearly exterminated as a people and we believe that it is important to keep our religion alive.

GUIDING QUESTION

Why is it important to understand the perspectives of the Ezidis?

PART SEVEN

GUIDING QUESTION

Why is it important to remember to do good things for others?

"How are you being treated in France as a refugee?" I asked.

"We are treated very kindly, like human beings. The people are very gracious to us. They offered us all the services that were possible. They helped my children register for school. I have four children between the ages of 10 and 16. It was very difficult for us at first because we did not know the French language at all. The first year was very stressful for all of us. We felt guilty for moving our children to a new country where they didn't understand the language.

But now the children are becoming acquainted with the French language. They understand enough of the language to be able to do their homework without assistance. They have met many French children who have welcomed them and become friends with them. Things are going very well for my children now.

Currently, I work for the French Red Cross full-time. I am really starting to enjoy my job quite a bit. It makes me happy to provide aid to other people who are coming to France from other countries. I enjoy that I get the opportunity to make people smile and feel relief. It's a good feeling."

"What is one final message that you have for American students?"

"You have a great nation. Keep your country strong and remember to help other communities."

GUIDING QUESTION

How does doing good things for others help Balsam to enjoy his new life in France?

A NOTE TO TEACHERS

Download the student reflection sheet and print it out for students to use in a think, pair, share activity. Before reading each section, discuss the section's guiding question with the class as a brainstorming activity and to activate prior knowledge. After reading each section, give students the opportunity to silently reflect by writing a response to the guiding question listed at the bottom of each section, onto their reflection sheet. After a few moments of reflection, to solidify what the students have learned, ask them to turn and share their thoughts with a student nearby. Once each group has shared with their partner(s), ask a few students to share out with the entire class. Then move onto the next section.

As a possible culminating activity, visit the NaTakallam website to request an hour-long zoom experience with a refugee from the Sinjar area of Iraq.

This is the link: https://natakallam.com/education/

Work with the students to create a list of culturally sensitive follow up questions regarding what the students are curious to learn more about. The opportunity to interact with a refugee is a priceless opportunity that will enhance empathy skills. Actually speaking with a person from Sinjar will foster a realization that the experiences of the Ezidi people are not nightmares, they are true stories of real human beings. Refugee stories are among the most tragic in the world, and their unique circumstances should be understood and respected.

STUDENT REFLECTION SHEET

How did a rumor destroy the reputation of the Ezidis?	
What form of propaganda was used to stir hate of the Ezidi people? If Iraqi children were more educated regarding forms of propaganda might the massacre of the Ezidis have been avoided or less widespread?	
How did the acceptance of the discrimination of the Ezidi people in Iraq ultimately lead to crimes against humanity?	
How did Saddam Hussein let his pride get in the way of doing what was best for his country?	
Considering the circumstances, should Ezidis return home and reclaim their villages, or move away?	
Why is it important to understand other people's perspectives?	
How does doing good things for others help Balsam to enjoy his new life in France?	

CHAPTER TWO

AN INTERVIEW WITH RAHIM
IRAQI WHO LIVED IN IRAN FOR 27 YEARS

PART ONE

VOCAB

Abu Ghraib Prison: "In the era of Saddam Hussein, Abu Ghraib, 20 miles west of Baghdad, was one of the world's most notorious prisons, with torture, weekly executions, and vile living conditions. As many as 50,000 men and women—no accurate count is possible—were jammed into Abu Ghraib at one time, in 12-by-12-foot cells that were little more than human holding pits" (The New Yorker).

Shia: "One of the two main branches of Islam, followed especially in Iran, that rejects the first three Sunni caliphs (religious leaders) and regards Ali, the fourth caliph, as Muhammad's first true successor" (Oxford Dictionary).

Sunni: "The larger of the two main branches of Islam, which differs from Shia. It believes that Abu Bakr was the rightful caliph, or religious leader, who took over when the Prophet Muhammad died" (Oxford Dictionary).

The Sunni and the Shia broke away from each other following the death of the Prophet Muhammad. The Sunnis believe that Abu Bakhr, the last person Muhammad asked to lead prayer, should take over as the next caliph. He was Muhammad's father-in-law and companion.

The Shia believe that Ali, Muhammad's cousin and son-in-law, should be the next caliph. He was also the only person that "was allowed to assist the Prophet in cleansing the Ka'ba for God" (Aslan 118). The Ka'ba is in Mecca and is the holiest sight of Islam. Muslims turn towards the Ka'ba to pray five times per day.

Sunni and Shia religious scholars continue to argue about who was the first rightful caliph, following Muhammad, to this day.

Kurd: An ethnic group of mostly Sunni Muslims, among them are many who practice Sufism and other mystical sects. The Kurds never achieved nation-state status.

Yezidi or Ezidi: "Yezidis is one of many religious minorities in Iraq. They follow Yezidism, a religion combining elements from, among others, Christianity and Islam. At the center is the teaching about a fallen angel who is forgiven by God and sent to govern the Earth in God's place." (The Norwegian refugee council). This belief led to their wrongful persecution as devil worshippers.

Christian: A major religion stemming from the life, teachings and death of Jesus of Nazareth. Christians are monotheistic and believe that Jesus is the son of God who was born, through a miracle, to the Virgin Mary. Christians believe in the Holy Trinity of God the Father, God the Son (Jesus) and the Holy Spirit. Christians believe that Jesus is the Messiah and he was crucified to redeem mankind and to open the gates of heaven. The Christian religion is the largest in the world and it dominates western nations as the predominant faith (britannica.com).

Saddam Hussein: President of Iraq from 1979-2003 when he was hanged by the American coalition forces following the second Gulf War.

Baathist Party: Saddam Hussein's political party. It was known for totalitarianism and brutality (pbs.org).

American Coalition: America and its 31 allies who went to war with Iraq including the UK, Australia, Spain, Poland and 26 others.

ISIS: The Islamic State of Iraq and Syria (britannica.com). A Sunni terrorist group that took over parts of western Iraq and eastern Syria. They are known for their brutality, including the beheading of the American journalist James Foley.

Take a moment to review the locations of Iraq and Iran on a map of the Middle East. Notice how close they are to each other. Also, notice Greece and Spain and their distance from Iraq. Iran, Greece and Spain are all locations that Rahim fled to at different stages of his life.

GUIDING QUESTIONS

*What are the benefits of being a citizen? (For example:
Citizens can vote, can work legally, can obtain a driver's
license and a passport.)*

*Why is it important for governments to respect differ-
ent cultures and religions?*

RAHIM'S STORY

Rahim left Iraq in 1983 when he was six months old. At
the time, his father was imprisoned and tortured in the
Abu Ghraib prison. His father is Shia. He landed in prison
because he attended some anti-government demonstrations;
but he was not a ringleader. He was simply in the wrong place
at the wrong time. Thus, he was detained for six months. He
was not executed; but the six months he spent in an Iraqi
prison left him scarred for life. When he was released he knew
that he needed to leave Iraq. The family chose to flee to Iran.

Sadaam Hussein and the Baathist Party were Sunni; this
party made every effort to subjugate the Shia majority in Iraq.
When the American coalition removed Saddam Hussein and
the Baathist Party from control in Iraq in 2003, Nouri al-Maliki
became the deputy leader of the Supreme National Debaathifi-
cation Commission of the Iraqi interim government (DW.com).
What Iraq truly needed was a government that would unite
the Sunni, Shia, Kurd and Yezidi. Unfortunately, the new Shia
government returned the treatment they had received from the
Sunni, and began subjugating them. Eventually, many of these
subjugated Sunni joined ISIS as a form of revenge.

While this was happening, Rahim and his family were in
Iran. They were being pressured to return home to Iraq because
the Shia were no longer being subjugated in Iraq; thus, it was

considered safe for them to return. Even though they had been living and working in Iran for 27 years, they never gained citizenship, and were expected to return home to Iraq as soon as it was safe to do so. In 2010, they returned to Iraq.

Rahim stayed in Iraq from 2010 until 2016 when he fled to Greece. He could not stay in Iraq because it is unacceptable to be an atheist there. His cousins, members in a Shia militia, reported him as an atheist to the authorities. The authorities went to his house at 4:00 in the morning to interrogate him. This scared him intensely. Thus, in 2016, he applied for a relocation program and made it to Spain by 2017. There he felt safe from the Shia militias.

Unfortunately, the Spanish authorities have argued that Rahim should return to Iraq where he can simply pretend to be Muslim; if he pretends to be Muslim he will not be murdered by the Shia militias there. When I interviewed Rahim, he was preparing for trial. His lawyer was arguing that Rahim is an atheist and he should not have to return to Iraq and pretend to be something that he is not, especially considering that if he was a Christian he would not be deported from Spain back to Iraq.

I interviewed Rahim on May 15, 2020:

Rahim has a gigantic smile and a wealth of knowledge. With each question I asked his eyes lit up. He was clearly moved that an American teacher wanted to share his story with the students of America. We met via Zoom on a beautiful March morning. He was in Spain; I was in the United States. We both began by discussing our personal experiences regarding COVID-19. I am teaching from home; he is working from home. Shortly thereafter I changed the topic to his home country, Iraq. I am curious about Sadaam Hussein's mistreatment of the Shia majority in Iraq. I begin with "why did Saddam Hussein ban Shia traditions in the 1980's?"

Through his thick accent and his large smile came an

abundance of fascinating insights. He smiled and said "Saddam Hussein did not want to share power. He wanted to oppress the Shia. He had the same plans for Kurds. So it is just basically, in my idea, it is basically just suppression; it's just discrimination against the other group that is not part of the government. These religious leaders were against the government so they didn't want the Shia people to be in contact with their religious leaders too much, or to listen to their religious leaders too much, because people may follow the words of the religious leaders rather than the words of the government. In my opinion, that was the main reason."

"Thank you." I went on, just to clarify, your theory is that Saddam Hussein was afraid that the Shia people would follow their religious leaders more than him? This is why he banned Shia traditions in Iraq?"

"Yes, that is correct."

"Thank you. I would like to spend a few minutes talking about why your family decided to flee Iraq and go to Iran."

"I went with my parents. They left Iraq in 1983. After Saddam Hussein took power, one of the first things he did was oppress the Shia. Then, for a limited amount of time, he gave them the freedom of pursuing their own religion and performing their own rituals. The Shia started doing their rituals in the streets. Those rituals started to change into demonstrations against the regime. Or the Shia would do the rituals in the streets, and at the end of the rituals they would do demonstrations against the regime.

My father was at one of the demonstrations. But my father wasn't the head of it or anything. He was at the demonstration and he was with a friend that was a little bit more active than him; but my father was just there doing his ritual as a devout Shia. He helped the man I mentioned who was his friend. This man was distributing sandwiches to people, and my father helped him because he needed a hand. He asked my father for help; so my father gave him a hand with distributing the sand-wiches. So they were hanging out the top of a car and giving out sandwiches to people.

The Baathist Regime Intelligence was there observing and they saw that my father was giving food to people and so the intelligence decided that the people giving out the sandwiches were the organizers. After the ritual ended they just came and arrested my father and they took him to Abu Ghraib prison. It was an infamous prison then; and it is infamous now. They tor-tured him a bit. They beat him up. They found his weak point. He is a very sympathetic person. He can't see blood. Even if he sees a very small amount of blood from a small cut he freaks out. The interrogations in this prison often were very bloody and sometimes they killed people during these interrogations. Well they assigned my father to be the cleaner of the interroga-tion room. My father had to clean the blood. Or, if the person was dead, my father had to collect the body. So my father was traumatized from that.

After six months, they just released him because, in the end, he wasn't an organizer. Besides the fact that he was on the top of the car giving out sandwiches, they couldn't find any addi-tional evidence, so they released him. He was traumatized and we were very worried that he would just get arrested again by the intelligence because the regime believed that my dad was somehow connected. It became obvious that it wasn't safe for my father, and my entire family, to live in Iraq anymore. As soon as my father was released my family collected everything. I was six months old and we fled the country to Iran.

There were two reasons why we decided to go to Iran. First, the path to Iran was open. The border was closed to every other country. There were a lot of Iraqis who had little to no family connection to Iran that were mass deported to Iran to put pressure on the new Islamic regime in Iran. There were about 2 to 3 million Iraqis that were just deported to Iran. These Iraqis were very devout Shia and most of them were against Saddam's regime. So Iraq decided to deport about 3 million Shia Iraqis to Iran to make a lesson of them and to end the problem of the Shia in Iraq. Since this path was open, and Iran was a Shia country, it was the easiest and the best destination for my father. We stayed in Iran for 27 years.

There is no path to citizenship in Iran, even if you are legally there. As soon as we arrived there we got refugee status; we were legally there. We were working there and legally residing there for 27 years. But there is no path to Iranian citizenship if you don't have an Iranian father. An Iranian mother would not be enough to get citizenship in Iran. After 20 years, in 2003, they told us that your reasons and your fears for being in Iran are not valid because the regime has changed in Iraq." (Saddam was gone. Shias were in control of the government because of the American invasion.)

"They didn't put a tremendous amount of pressure on us to move back to Iraq. But they were always reminding us that we should go back to Iraq. But Iraq was unstable between 2003 and 2010. We waited until 2010 to go back to Iraq." He paused and I responded to him with sympathy.

"It must have been very difficult for you to have grown up in Iran for 27 years while it was always expected that you would go home to Iraq. I'm sure neither country really ever felt like your own country. The Sunnis and the Shias have been at odds since the death of the Prophet Muhammad when they disagreed over who should take over as caliph. It seems this ongoing dispute caused you to be disconnected from your home country."

GUIDING QUESTIONS

What would it feel like to live in a country, from the time you were six months old, but the country would never grant you citizenship? What emotions might you have?

How might Rahim's life have been different if Saddam Hussein respected different cultures and religions?

PART TWO

VOCAB

Deradicalization: "The process of encouraging a person with extreme political, social or religious views to adopt a more moderate approach" (Wikipedia).

Al-Qaeda: The Islamic fundamentalist group responsible for Sept. 11th.

Proxy war: A way of avoiding direct conflict by aiding an enemy's enemy.

NGOs: Non-governmental organizations such as Doctors Without Borders which works to provide medical assistance to people affected by war, epidemics and natural disasters or and Amnesty International which prevents human rights abuses.

GUIDING QUESTION

Why is the de-radicalization of captured terrorists critical to the future of the world?

"Rahim, do you think there will always be a conflict between the Sunni and Shia?"

"That's a good question", Rahim began. "Actually I think so. When I stepped back and I decided not to be a Muslim, and I started looking at the situation with more objectivity, I realized that there are two main sources of today's conflict. The first is the proxy war between Iran and Saudi Arabia, happening in Iraq. I don't believe it will end anytime soon. Iran backs the Shia militias in Iraq; and Saudi Arabia backs the Sunnis there. Before the second Gulf War, there were Sunni militias and Shia militias. But now because the majority of the government is Shia, the Sunni militias are classified as illegal, and now they are labeled 'terrorists'. So the conflict in Iraq is a result of the proxy war between Iran and Saudi Arabia, and it will not end soon."

His face appeared authentically disheartened as he went on. "The other reason for the Sunni-Shia conflict is the incompetence of the Iraqi government in resolving the problems in the conflict areas and putting together any plan for healing the radicalization of the people. There is no plan for that and actually no cooperation from the government with all the NGOs (Non-Governmental Organizations) and the Red Cross.

The Sunnis were pushed back from the political process in Iraq after the second Gulf War. The results of that were Al-Qaeda and then ISIS. Al-Qaeda built bases in Iraq. The lack of education in that area led to oppression and resulted in radicalization. People there started backing ISIS. So what happened is after (Rahim made quotation mark motions with his fingers) 'defeating ISIS' the Iraqi government moved all the families of the former ISIS fighters to areas in Kurdistan, and put them in camps, with little or no connection to the outside. There was no plan to de-radicalize them or to re-integrate them. So those camps in the north of Iraq became hotspots for radicalization because there was no plan. I can't stress that enough.

The western area of Iraq where ISIS had control is still impoverished. The tribes there, under the pressure of the Iraqi government, decided to make a tribal sentence for all of these families of the ISIS fighters. The tribes decided to expel them from the western community for ten years. So these families that we moved from the western area to the north in the camps, the tribes will not accept them to come back for the next ten years. So these people, and their relatives, will be radicalized even more against the tribes and against the Iraqi government. What happened is that there became a very fertile field for radicalization in the camps and there is no plan for solving the problem. I don't see any variable changing right now, especially with the proxy war on top of it. I believe this is because Saudi Arabia would love the radicalization in the Sunni areas and Iran would love the radicalization in the Shia areas. In the end, these countries are just putting gasoline on the top of the fire. This problem will come back sooner or later."

GUIDING QUESTION

Why is de-radicalization of captured terrorists critical to the future of the world?

PART THREE

VOCAB

Embargo: "Legal prohibition by a government or group of governments resisting the departure of vessels or movement of goods from some or all locations to one or more countries" (Britannica).

Sanctions: "Actual or threatened punishments: for example refusing to export, refusing to import, refusing to trade" (Britannica). Starting in 1990, the United Nations Security Council imposed sanctions on Iraq that were seen as the toughest in UN history. By severely limiting Iraq's ability to import or export goods the economy, and thus, the people suffered greatly.

Kuwait: The small country south of Iraq. This country was part of Iraq under the administrative rule of the Ottoman Empire. As the victors of World War I, Britain and France demolished the Ottoman Empire. "Britain blocked Iraq's access to the Persian Gulf by severing it from Kuwait in 1921. (Klein). Saddam believed Iraq deserved to take Kuwait back; he also accused neighboring Kuwait of violating its border and stealing "$2.4 billion worth of Iraqi oil at the border" (Rethinking Schools).

Totalitarian: "Form of government that prohibits individual freedom and seeks to subordinate all aspects of individual life to the authority of the state" (Britannica).

Frankenstein: A scientist who created a monster that eventually killed him. "This monster later befriends a young girl in the nearby countryside but then inadvertently drowns her in a lake. Eventually, a village mob forms and traps the monster in an abandoned windmill, which the mob then sets ablaze, apparently destroying the monster" (Britannica).

GUIDING QUESTION

Imagine that the UN was angry with your government for refusing to allow UN weapons inspectors to inspect nuclear facilities in your country. The UN decided to restrict trade until your government made a change. Your parents lost their jobs at the local factory because of the economic sanctions. What types of feelings might you have about the UN and your government officials?

My next question is what are your thoughts about the UN embargo, or refusal to trade with Iraq, from in the early 1990's and until 2001?"

"So that is very interesting. You know sometimes when I think about this stuff it just breaks my heart, you know? Because when Saddam Hussein took over in Iraq and started the war against Iran... Do you know the story of Frankenstein?"

"Yes, the monster who killed the scientist who created him," I responded.

"Yes, so you know the Frankenstein monster?"

"Yes, I know the Frankenstein monster, yes."

"That's basically what happened in regards to Saddam Hussein. Around the time when Saddam Hussein took power there was an Islamic revolution in Iran that the US was completely against. Saddam Hussein, out of nowhere, decided to attack Iran. There are a lot of arguments there that the US government, and Arab governments in the area, kind of supported him or pushed him into that war. So he entered that war with Iran and there were no sanctions against him for starting that war with Iran. The war continued for eight years. There was nothing against Saddam Hussein for doing that. When they ended the war there was no prosecution, nothing, no sanctions, nothing against Saddam Hussein."

His face appeared frustrated as he continued. "What happened is two years after that war ended, Saddam Hussein attacked Kuwait. He (Rahim makes quotation marks in the air) 'appended' Kuwait to the country with little to no resistance for a very long time." (Saddam Hussein invaded on August 2, 1990. The US attacked Iraq on January 17, 1991.)

"Then they started the war against him. Saddam Hussein was arrogant of course. All the totalitarian government leaders are arrogant... So he was arrogant. Saddam decided now I'm going to attack Kuwait and there were a lot of other discussions, or other documents, or other conclusions that came out saying that Saddam Hussein actually got a greenlight from the US to attack Kuwait. But then the US defeated him and put him under sanctions for ten years; half a million children died as a result of the sanctions, and suddenly they attacked in 2003.

After 13 years nothing changed- from 1991 when the first Gulf War happened until 2003, nothing changed in Iraq. There were no weapons of mass destruction and America didn't find them.

Concerning your question, no I completely disagree with what happened in that time with the decision of the US to sanction Iraq because I know people, I had relatives in Iraq. I wasn't in Iraq, I had moved to Iran by then, but my relatives in Iraq suffered from absolute poverty and lack of medical care. At the end of the day when you put the government under pressure, what happens is the poorest of the poor pay the price. This is happening in Iran now. The government will do whatever it wants to do and the poor are getting poorer and poorer. The government is totalitarian, so it doesn't care."

"Was it mostly the Shia that suffered under the sanctions in

Iraq, and not the Sunni?" I asked. I'm assuming that Saddam didn't really care as much about the Shia as long as the Sunnis and his close friends were eating well?"

"Well only a small part of the Sunnis benefited to be honest, to be fair. The people who were close to him, and the people who were connected to him were eating well. There were a lot of Sunnis that did not benefit from the situation."

"Right, I had heard that Saddam used the sanctions to his advantage. Since Iraq couldn't trade, and the resources became so scarce, he kept the people close to him loyal because if they were disloyal they would starve like the rest of the country."

GUIDING QUESTION

The sanctions on Iraq broke Rahim's heart. Many Iraqis had to move to smaller homes and sell their furniture. They went without electricity for several hours a day and only one of the children in each family could typically go to school. (Iraqi Muslims usually have around five or six children.) Their parents were too ashamed to send all of their children because they could not afford shoes, clothes and backpacks for more than one child. What types of feelings were stirred in the Iraqi people living under the sanctions? Who did they most likely blame?

PART FOUR

VOCAB

Power Vacuum: "A condition that exists when someone has lost control of something, such as a government, and no one has replaced them" (Cambridge Dictionary).

Baghdad: The capital of Iraq

Sovereignty: "The authority of a state to govern itself." (Britannica)

GUIDING QUESTION

Who typically wins and who typically loses in wars?

My next question for Rahim was "what are your thoughts about the United States' decision to take Saddam Hussein out of power?"

Rahim responded with a serious tone. "Before I answer the question, I want to remind you that we were in another country, Iran. My family and I were refugees and we were in a very difficult situation because of Saddam Hussein. My family was in Iran because of Saddam Hussein. If I say anything negative about Saddam Hussein it is because I am a little bit biased. If I say something positive I hope that you accept it from me because my father was tortured for six months in jail under Saddam Hussein."

He continued with a look of acceptance. "What I'm saying is, yes, Saddam Hussein was a horrible person. He was a tyrant. He was a war criminal. He was a mass murderer and everyone knows that. However, after overthrowing Saddam Hussein there was a vacuum of power and this led a radicalized group to seize power in Iraq; and it started chaos. Between 2003 and 2008 there were 1 million Iraqis that died as a result of the war and the activities and operations of the radicalized group that had the freedom to operate in the absence of a real government. The result was chaotic. The government is still suffering from that result. The number of people in poverty did not change much. The basic services that the government was not providing to the people such as electricity are still not being provided to the people. The infrastructure of the government was destroyed before 2003, with the invasion there was no rebuilding of that infrastructure happening in Iraq. The people are suffering from lack of electricity. They have three hours of electricity and then three hours of a generator in their homes. They just put some petrol in the generator and just start it up to have some electricity in the houses. There is no clean water available in some areas.

I would not describe Baghdad as a safe city for everybody. Also, we can all agree that the west of Iraq is also not safe. So the entire country is not safe because if one part of the country is not safe then the entire country is not safe. After all, whatever happens in one part is going to affect the other parts of the country. At the end of the day it's one country. We don't have safety, we don't have electricity, and we don't have water. We don't have good education. We don't have medical facilities to provide medical assistance to people. We don't have equipped hospitals.

In Baghdad, the *Red Cross* is operating to give some basic day-to-day needs. So nothing has changed for people. Just more people have died. At the end of the day Iraq turned from a country with sovereignty to an area of a proxy war between different countries. It was just a plan to invade Iraq at any cost. They invaded it and there was no exit plan. There was no plan whatsoever, just invade, overthrow the government, and then figure out what happens. We pay the price. The Iraqi people and the American soldiers that went there and fought and died paid the price. Everyone lost, from my perspective, everyone lost."

I asked a follow-up question. "Do you think we would have been better off if we did not take Saddam Hussein out of power?"

"That's a good question. I'm saying that it didn't get better. But the thing is there are a lot of actors, and difficult actors."

"Yes that's very true," I agreed.

"I will argue that at least for the first five years it was worse. At least for the first five years it was way, way worse."

GUIDING QUESTION

According to Rahim, who were the winners and who were the losers in the Second Gulf War? Why?

PART FIVE

VOCAB

AAH: Asaib Ahl al-Haqor AKA League of Righteous- Shia militant group. It wants Iraq to be a Shia controlled state. It also wants "to expel the remaining US military and diplomatic presence from the country."(- understandingwar.org). It has been known for recruiting disenfranchised Iraqi youths and sending them to Iran for training with Hezbollah. They are known for using mortars, rockets, kidnappings, snipers and other tactics.

One example of their brutality is when they "kidnapped British computer consultant Peter Moore to exchange with Iraqi prisoners taken by Britain but held by the United States" (The Guardian). He was tortured. His four bodyguards were killed. He was released after 31 months.

Prophet Muhammad: The final and most important messenger of God's words to the Muslim religion. Muslims believe he received the word of God directly from the Angel Gabriel. The messages Muslims believe he received are written in the Qur'an.

GUIDING QUESTION

Why is it important for a country to be united?

"Can we talk about present-day Iraq for a bit? Would you be concerned for your safety, as an atheist, if you were to return to Iraq considering all the different militia groups that are present in the country?"

"That's a very good question. There is a militia group in Iraq. They call it AAH. They are the most radicalized militia in Iraq. When I left in 2016 they were recruiting and recruiting. They were strong. They weren't as strong as they are now. In 2018 when the war happened against ISIS, the US allowed all militias to help the government in defeating ISIS. So what happened is that AAH gained more popularity among people. AAH helped in defeating ISIS so they had more popularity. The result of the popularity is that they ended up getting members in Parliament. I consider the AAH to be a terrorist group. This group now has members in the Iraqi Parliament and thus, more power.

I was talking to my brother, who still lives in Iraq, and he said that now they have much more popularity than they did before defeating ISIS. If I go back to Iraq of course I cannot go to the Sunni areas because my parents are Shia so sooner or later because of my last name, or my place of birth, or my documents they will understand and they will see that I am Shia, so they might kill me. Also, I cannot live in Kurdistan because I am Arab and the rules are that if you are Arab you cannot just live in the north of Iraq. I don't know why but this is the situation in Iraq. They don't want Arabs to live in Kurdistan. The Kurds want to have a real Kurdish state there. And, when I go to the Shia areas, it is controlled by the militias. The militias have popularity, freedom, and weapons. So I'm really concerned about being sent back to Iraq. I'm really afraid that my life would be in more danger now than it was when I left in 2016 because I am an atheist and I was intimidated into leaving then because the militias see atheism as an insult to the Prophet Muhammad. So they entered my home in the middle of the night and threatened me and my entire family.

Rahim looks down in sadness. But then he looks up with a smile. "However, I had luck. I was a little bit lucky. I found the love of my life. I got engaged in Europe and she has Italian nationality and as a spouse of a European national they cannot deport me to my home country so...." Rahim gets a large smile on his face and turns bright red. He goes on to say "I can promise you that I didn't start my relationship because I didn't want to get deported. At the time when I started my relationship there was a better chance that I would get status in Europe."

"Congratulations! I am so happy for you that you are in love and that you will be safe! May I ask, what in particular scares you most about the AAH?"

"For my own situation or for the country?"

"Both would be helpful."

"OK, I will answer for myself while summarizing the story of AAH. The thing is AAH tried to define itself to people as a guardian of the people and of their religion. Iraq is a heavily Muslim country. Religion is very apparent everywhere. It is all over, in every aspect of life. Unfortunately, in Iraq we don't have a sense of nationality. A lot of Iraqis say that they don't have a sense of nationality. We don't express ourselves as Iraqis. For example, if I was Shia then I would say that I am Shia; I would not say that I am Iraqi. Further, someone in the south of Iraq would not accept that someone in the west of Iraq has the same rights as he does. Instead, they say I am Shia and he is Sunni; and the other guy is Kurd. This is a characteristic of a defeated nation. The people don't want to characterize it as a nation. They believe that they acted in the defeat of Iraq differently. They believe that the other groups are the facilitators of the defeat. For example, the Sunnis say that the Shia opened the doors for the Americans to invade the country. The Shia say that it was the suppression of Saddam Hussein that made America invade. The Kurds blame both groups. This is what is happening in Iraq. It is very apparent that everyone is defining themselves with their ethnicity and especially with their religion. Whoever can serve the idea that they are the guardian of the religion, and there is a war against your religion, and I am the guardian of your religion, and I am the protector of the religion, will gain a lot of popularity in that area.

If someone like me, out of nowhere, starts questioning, not only the militias, but also the religion, and the very basis of the religion, what will happen is they define me as an 'enemy of the people' and an 'enemy of God', or the religion, and they execute me."

GUIDING QUESTION

Why is it important for a country to be united?

PART SIX

VOCAB
Constitution: The higher law of the land.

GUIDING QUESTION
What are the benefits of separation of church and state?

"Rahim," I began, "Is there no separation of church and state in Iraq?"

Rahim smiled and I could see through his expression that he was realizing how different our societies are. He did his best to explain. "The Iraqi constitution is not very clear. The Iraqi constitution says the Iraqi penal codes are aligned with Islam. Thus, there is a problem here. If a religious Shia leader ruled to kill someone because of Islam, but according to constitutional law the person is not considered guilty, the law is not clear on what is right because the constitution is aligned with Islam. For example, in the early 2000's there was an Iraqi who killed his father because the father was a translator for the American army in Iraq. So he killed his father and they jailed this guy; but they couldn't prosecute him because he acted as a good Muslim, because he received the fatwa." (A fatwa is a decree handed down by an Islamic religious leader.)

"The fatwa said that his father should be executed. He executed his own father because he wanted to be a good Muslim. Do you see what is happening? The thing is the religious leaders are completely aligned with these militias because whenever they get information, they get it from the militias.

So, in my particular situation, I wasn't only questioning the religion; I was questioning the very fact that it makes no sense to have a militia instead of one strong army to defeat ISIS. Why do we need to have a militia to go and fight?

In Iraq we have ISIS, and we have families of ISIS members. But if we have a government, then we will have a system to deal with it. If we have a group of people who have weapons and are religiously motivated to kill people then we don't know what will happen there and usually what happens is war crimes. There are a lot of good media that published the war crimes that were happening, like Reuters published some of the war crimes that were happening by the militias to the families of the ISIS members. Let's not forget, being a relative of an ISIS member is not a crime. Being an ISIS member is a crime. But being a family member of a person that is in ISIS, or even if you morally support ISIS, that is not a crime. Unless you kill people, or you do violent things to other people, it is not a crime. But the militias prosecuted people or killed people because they were family members of ISIS.

In my particular case, I am sure that they would take the matter into their own hands and that they would kill me if I returned home to Iraq. This would be justified because they would justify killing me by labeling me as an enemy of God and religion because I am an atheist. This would give more authority to the people and more popularity to AAH or other groups, and so they would execute me if I returned home. In Islam, we have a saying that whoever strikes doubt in the heart of the believers is an enemy of God. How do you interpret that?"

"Wow," I responded. "That is very scary. Anyone who strikes doubt in the heart of others is an enemy. That is very scary if it is interpreted by someone who wants to harm atheists. It seems they can use this as an excuse."

"Yeah, whatever you say, you're spreading the doubt", was his reply.

"I'm so sorry that this is the situation you are in; you cannot return to your home country because you are afraid that they will kill you."

GUIDING QUESTION

What problems arise from the lack of separation of church and state in Iraq?

PART SEVEN

GUIDING QUESTION

Is the enemy of my enemy my friend?

"Rahim, I would like to ask you more about AAH. As you know they did 6,000 attacks on the coalition (US, UK Australia, Spain, Poland, and others) forces. This being said, what was the aftermath of these attacks and did they affect you at all?

"Well, I can only answer you from my own experience. AAH is deeply connected to Iran. Don't forget that before 2003 Saddam Hussein had complete power. His regime had people working for him from each community. So there were members of the Baathist Party that were Shia, even though Saddam was Sunni, and they were working for Saddam Hussein in the Shia areas. They were very high ranked. The Baathist Party members, who were Shia, were not put on the coalition members' list of people to hunt down after they took Saddam Hussein out of power. Only the Sunni ones were put on the list. So these Baathist members, who are Shia, gathered together and eventually became known as the AAH. A lot of Shia did not like Saddam Hussein; but they did not like the invasion as well. So instead they started to support AAH. This group started getting bigger and bigger and bigger; and they started attacking the coalition as well. They continued to attack them. Eventually, they were put on the terrorist list. But in Iraq, in the southern area, nothing happened to them, to be honest."

"That is interesting!," I responded, "So what you are saying is the Shia who worked for Hussein, even though Hussein was Sunni, became a large part AAH and they never suffered any consequences for working with Hussein or for any attacks on the coalition forces?"

"Yes, and now they (AAH) have popularity. They have weapons. No one is prosecuting them. They are working with the government. Iraqi government officials have big, big sympathy or empathy with AAH. They report to these groups. They give information or intelligence to these groups. I would argue that nothing happened to AAH. They were there. They got more popular. They became more powerful and actually in 2018 they attacked ISIS. They became a part of the coalition that was fighting ISIS and participated. Also, the entire coalition got the gratitude of Mr. Pompeo, the secretary of state. He thanked AAH very much for their help fighting ISIS."

"So what you're saying is that groups that we labeled as terrorists, groups that had attacked the coalition, such as AAH, we later praised for their support in our fight against ISIS? Well, I guess it's a classic case of the enemy of my enemy is my friend.

GUIDING QUESTION

AAH was the enemy of ISIS; did that make them the friend of the Iraqi government or the US? Should the US have fought alongside them against ISIS? Should the Iraqi soldiers have fought alongside them?

PART EIGHT

VOCAB

Badr Corps: Formed in 2003. It wanted revenge against the Sunni Baathist party for its mistreatment of the Shia under Saddam Hussein. They are known for kidnappings, executions and extortions.

Iran-Iraq War: (1980-1988) Saddam Hussein, a Sunni, invaded its neighboring Shia country.

GUIDING QUESTION

Why is it important for governments to provide services to its people? (Examples: vaccinations, police, fire, etc.)

"Rahim, can you talk a bit about Badr Corps? What did they do that was beneficial, or detrimental?"

"That is a very interesting question. Thank you so much for asking. This relates directly to my situation even before my family returned from Iran to Iraq in 2010. That group was built by Iran, in Iran, by the Iraqi soldiers that had been arrested. It was made up of the Iraqi soldiers who surrendered to Iran during the Iran-Iraq War. There are so many soldiers from Iraq that just surrendered because they were Shia, and Iran is Shia, and they didn't want to fight against their own, so they surrendered. Or when Iran captured soldiers, a lot of them were Shia and they were there because Saddam Hussein forced them to be there. In Iran there was a man named Mohammad Bakr al-Hakim. He went to the government. He was a religious leader. He argued that Iran should use the soldiers that are rotting in the prisons. He argued to release them because they

like the Iranian government better than the Iraqi government
and they want to serve Iran. He argued to mobilize them as
soldiers who can fight for Iran.

In the beginning Iran wasn't sure about that. But then when
they released the prisoners, and promised them a better life,
they mobilized and organized and formed this Badr Group.
They were, at the time, called the Badr Army. In the last year
or two of the Iran-Iraq War there was an operation from Iraq
into Iran that this army went and fought; and the Badr Group
stopped that Iraqi operation. They became so connected
to Iran that they completely aligned themselves with Iran's
government.

After 2003, and the power vacuum in Iraq, the Badr Group
became more powerful in the south of Iraq and they declared
their support to the main religious leader in Iraq, Ayatollah
Ali al-Sistani. Some people see the Badr Group as the saviors
of the Shia people in Iraq against the remainder of Saddam
Hussein's Baathist Regime. Later on they were seen as Shia
saviors against Al-Qaeda.

They were doing what the National Revolutionary Guard
in Iran was doing. They were essentially part of the National
Revolutionary Guard. So forgive me if you don't know what the
National Revolutionary Guard is in Iran. In Iran they have two
major armies. They have the army and they have the National
Revolutionary Guard. The National Revolutionary Guard has
more power than the army and it is involved in politics as well.
They are the main arm of the supreme leader and do whatever
he wants in Iran. So this is the main power in Iran. They are
the main oppressors who run the country. They have a lot of
political and economic interest in Iran. The Badr Group was a
part of the National Revolutionary Guard.

In the beginning, the National Revolutionary Guard got
the support of the Iranians by going into the poor areas and

providing services for people. For example, they provided vaccinations to domestic animals and vaccinations for children. They also provided specific programs to fertilize the agricultural fields. They started helping people with that. The things that the government of Iran should've been doing, the National Revolutionary Guard did because they were more organized than the government. Since they were providing services, they earned popularity among the people. The National Revolutionary Guard started to get more and more members. So now that they had a lot of members, a lot of people knew someone who worked for them. For example, if my brother was working for the National Revolutionary Guard I would not say anything negative about them because my brother was working for them. They extended their ties to people and to everyone in this way in the 80's and in the 90's.

The Badr Group learned from them. They actually came after my father. They said 'since you're a refugee would you like to come work for us? We will give you a better job and a better salary.' They also told him 'if one day Saddam Hussein goes away, and we overthrow him, you will get a good result out of it. We will make sure that you have a good job with good compensation.' But my father rejected this. He refused to work for them; so he spent his life as a worker in a textile factory.

The Badr Group moved to Iraq and they started going into the poor areas and doing the same things that the National Revolutionary Guard did for people in Iran. They provided vaccinations and medical aid. They helped the farmers in rural areas. They ran checkpoints to see if people had guns. They were trained by the Iranian Intelligence Service; they were good at what they did. They were taking care of the intelligence that Iraq should've done; but the Iraqi government was destroyed at the time. So they started providing the services; but the thing is, the leaders of that group did not support the building of an intelligence service in Iraq. They were benefiting from the fact that there was a lack of strong intelligence in Iraq. They had more freedom to do whatever they wanted without being held accountable, even in the Sunni areas. In general, they provided aid that the government should've been doing; but in return they blocked any attempt to build the part of the government that should've been responsible for these services. They benefited hugely from it. Now they have a huge amount of weapons. They are not doing much in the way of providing services anymore. They are mostly doing intelligence and attacks in the Sunni areas." He smiles.

"That was a very long answer," he remarks.

"That was excellent," I responded. "It clarified a lot. If I may, are you personally afraid of the Badr Corps?"

"To be honest we have a lot to fear in Iraq. I was more afraid of AAH than the Badr Group, to be honest, because they are more radicalized and organized right now. They have Parliament members now. But the Badr Corps is bad. Both groups are bad. But for me I am more afraid of AAH. Let's say that Badr Corps is like a close second."

GUIDING QUESTION

How did the Badr Corps take advantage of the fact that the Iraqi government was unable to provide many services to its people?

PART NINE

VOCAB

VPNs: Using a VPN to connect to the internet allows anyone the ability to surf websites privately and securely and to gain access to restricted websites while overcoming censorship blocks.

Green Wave: "On June 23, 2009, a spontaneous mass demonstration erupted in Iran against the most publicly contested presidential election in the history of the Islamic Republic.... On June 25, Iran witnessed a huge mass rally against the status quo with the slogan of 'Where is My Vote?', which eventually emerged as the defining moment of an uprising that its supporters now call the 'Green Movement.'" (Al Jazeera).

GUIDING QUESTION

Should social media be regulated under any circumstances?

"Can you talk about the Iranian government's decision to block Twitter and other forms of social media? Why does the Iranian government think that this is a good idea since a lot of Iranians cheat the system and use Twitter anyway?"

"That's a very good question. The first social media blocking happened in 2009. I was in Iran at that time and they blocked Facebook. Before 2008 or 2009 only pornographic websites were blocked. In 2009, if you remember, there was an election in Iran. The majority of the people, including me, wanted a new president. There was a big movement because there was a president there that was not representing the people and the people wanted to change the president.

The thing is that in Iran they don't have a very democratic system. This president was not popular; his last name was Ahmadinejad. People went by the millions, even people who had never voted before in their lives, went and voted against him. But the government just cheated. The day after they released the results of the election there was an uprising in Iran and this resulted in the Green Wave. Ahmadinejad won the election but the citizens did not believe that it was real.

It was a pro democratic wave that started in 2009; but it was crushed in 2009 as well. The people who were marching in the streets were connecting and organizing through Facebook. Before 2009 people didn't really know what Facebook was in Iran. Suddenly they said 'let's organize. How can we organize?' They started using Facebook. They couldn't use text messages because texting was controlled, or it was expensive, so they used Facebook. And then the government blocked Facebook and Twitter to try to control the uprising.

The VPNs started then. But they weren't VPNs; they were websites that if you wanted to unblock a website you would go to that website. There's a search engine where you could put the address of the blocked website in it, and hit search, and it would open that website as a proxy on that page. It was very difficult. Little by little people started producing and selling VPNs and it became possible to anonymously use social media.

I responded with an understanding tone. "That makes sense because I have seen Iranians on Twitter."

His face lit up with something more he wanted to talk about. "I actually analyzed the tweets on Twitter regarding General Soleimani's assassination," he explained. "Even though Twitter is blocked in Iran, I pulled the data on Twitter of people who were using a popular hashtag about General Soleimani's assassination by the United States. The sentiment that I gathered among Iranians was more than 60% of the tweets were from people supporting the Iranian government, in Persian. Persians usually don't use social media to put their ideas forward because they are afraid that the government will find them and arrest them. The funny thing is that most of the people who were using that hashtag about him were supporting the government and trying to send a message to the US that we are going to have a hard revenge.

I found it ridiculous though because to support the government of Iran on Twitter you had to break the blockage of that website, which is, according to the law of Iran, illegal. So it is illegal to use the VPN. So they were using a VPN to illegally support the government. This is a very funny thing that I witnessed."

GUIDING QUESTION

Should social media be regulated under any circumstances?

PART TEN

VOCAB

Qasem Soleimani: "An Iranian major general and commander of the Qudz force, a wing of the Islamic Revolutionary Guard Corps responsible for foreign operations" (Britannica). He was known for working with Hezbollah, which is designated as a terrorist organization by a large portion of the international community against what he viewed as Jewish aggression in Israel. He was assassinated under the Trump administration in 2020.

Islamic National Revolutionary Guard: Established under Ayatollah Ruhollah Khomeini and made up of well-trained fighters that the new Islamic republic of 1979 "knew were committed to guarding Iran's new political system and the ideals of the Islamic revolution" (The Washington Post).

Israel: The nation of Israel is a Jewish nation that was established for Jews following the Holocaust. The Jews see it as a necessary refuge for Jews. If Jews have their own Jewish nation, they believe there could never be a Holocaust again. The land of Israel was selected by the UN because the Jews also believe that this land was promised to them by God in the Old Testament of the Bible. Jerusalem is the holiest city for the Jews and it is the city where they believe the Ark of the Covenant was housed. The Ark was in the Holy Holies which is inside the Dome of the Rock today. This is the place Jews believe is the spiritual junction of heaven and earth and it is the direction Jews face when they pray. The Ark held Moses' staff, the mana, or everlasting food the Jews ate while traveling out of bondage from Egypt to Israel, and the 10 Commandment Tablets, according to the Jews and Christians.

When the Jewish nation was created many Palestinians were displaced. The Palestinian people refer to this as the Nakba, or catastrophe. Many Palestinians still believe that they have the right to return to the homeland of their ancestors. Also, in the 1967 Six-Day War, the Jews took territories from Jordan and Egypt. These territories are the West Bank, which they took from Jordan, and the Gaza Strip, which they took from Egypt. These territories are predominately Palestinian territories and have been under Israeli occupation ever since. Palestinians living in these territories live under Israeli control but do not have the right to vote. Groups like Hamas in the Gaza Strip, and Hezbollah in the West Bank, often use violent measures to try to fight for the right of return, and other Palestinian causes. There is an ongoing conflict in Israel between the Palestinians and the Jews over this territory. The Jews built a wall separating the Jews from the Palestinian territories and have been known for arbitrarily arresting Palestinians, denying them access to parks and beaches, and shooting protesters. Iran supports the Palestinians in their struggle.

GUIDING QUESTIONS

How can politicians use our fears to gain our support?

Why is voting important?

"Can you talk about General Qasem Soleimani for a bit?", I asked.

"Yes. He was from Iran but most of his operations were outside of Iran. He was a member of the National Revolutionary Guard. As a member, he was assigned several different positions, and some of them were internal. The National Revolutionary Guard is well organized and well-connected.

I can talk about him from an Iranian point of view and then also from my point of view as an Iraqi. As an Iraqi, I will say a lot of things that happened in Iraq as a proxy war, and a lot of people who died in Iraq as a proxy war, were a result of the operations that were carried out by him, and through his guidance. He should have taken some responsibility for the people who died in Iraq. Of course, he did not have the best interest of the Iraqi people in his heart. He was doing whatever he or the supreme leader wanted him to do in Iraq which does not have anything to do with the best interest of the Iraqi people. I would argue that he is a war criminal and a mass murderer.

In 2018 when they defeated Daesh (ISIS) the Shia militias had fought Daesh (ISIS) with the Iraqi government, the Iraqi military, and the American coalition as well. They were fighting alongside each other with one enemy. Soleimani fought with the Americans and the Iraqi government against ISIS.

But in 2019 when there was an uprising against the Iraqi regime because of the lack of services, and the corruption of the government, the people wanted the Prime Minister (Adil Abdul-Mahdi) to step down. Qasim Soleimani went to Iraq to meet with the Prime Minister who was ready to step down; but after meeting with Qasim Soleimani the Prime Minister decided not to step down. Everyone was saying that Soleimani talked him out of stepping down and convinced him to crush the demonstrators instead. As a result, thousands of protesters died before the Prime Minister decided to step down in 2019. As an Iraqi person I can say I hate Qasam Soleimani for this.

Iranians have mixed feelings about Qasim Soleimani. The majority of them hate the government and they hate the National Revolutionary Guard. However, they are afraid of Israel as well. The government did a great job in portraying

Qasim Soleimani as a hero before he was assassinated because he was on the front line fighting with Israel. Iran has portrayed Israel, alongside America, as their number one enemy. Iranians are not as decisive about Qasim Soleimani as they are decisive about the regime. 80% of Iranians hate the regime, I would estimate. But probably only about 50% agreed with Soleimani's policies because he was fighting Israel and he argued that if you don't fight Israel in Lebanon and Palestine, Israel will eventually come to Iran and invade. So Qasem Soleimani was a hero that was keeping Israel and America away from Iran, keeping them away from their family, and keeping them safe.

When it comes to his assassination I would say most Iranians disagreed with his assassination. Not because they liked him but because, in their minds, there are two irresponsible governments, the Iranian government that proved to be very irrational and the current US government (He was referring to the Trump administration) that proved to be very impulsive. They were afraid of war. They were afraid that a war might happen and the whole country might burn. If war happened Iranians thought that their children, economy, jobs, health system, and everything else in Iran would be burnt. Most Iraqis and Iranians disagreed with the assassination because they were afraid of a war which luckily didn't happen; but they are really afraid that it might." Rahim paused and I responded to his thoughts.

"It appears that most Iranians and most Americans have that in common; we do not want to go to war'" I said. Then I asked my final question. "Do you have one final message for American students?"

"Young Americans are the voters of tomorrow, and their votes not only can change the future of the United States, but also could determine the future of other countries. Just like the voters in 2001, in America, had more influence on the future of my country, than my father."

GUIDING QUESTIONS

How did Qasem Soleimani use the Iranian people's fears to gain their support?

2) How important is the American vote to Rahim?

PRINTABLE WORKSHEET FOR TEACHERS

Guiding Questions	Answer before reading the section	Answer after reading the section*
Part 1: What are the benefits of being a citizen?		
Why is it important for governments to respect different cultures and religions?		
Part 2: Why is de-radicalization of captured terrorists critical to the future of the world?		
Part 3: Imagine that the UN was angry with your government for refusing to allow UN weapons inspectors to inspect nuclear facilities in your country. The UN decided to restrict trade until your government made a change. Your parents lost their jobs at the local factory because of the economic sanctions. What types of feelings might you have about the UN and your government officials?		

*   Guiding questions are sometimes reworded at the end of the sections. Use a quote from the text to support each of your responses.

Guiding Questions	Answer before reading the section	Answer after reading the section'
Part 4: Who typically wins and who typically loses in wars?		
Part 5: Why is it important for a country to be united?		
Part 6: What are the benefits of separation of church and state?		
Part 7: Is the enemy of my enemy my friend?		
Part 8: Why is it important for governments to provide services to its people? (Examples: vaccinations, police, fire, etc.)		
Part 9: Should social media be regulated under any circumstances?		
Part 10: How can politicians use our fears to gain our support?		
Part 10: Why is voting important?		

CHAPTER THREE

MALIKA AND MOHAMMAD FROM AFGHANISTAN

After the Sept 11th attacks, and 20 years of American dedication to freeing Afghanistan from the Taliban, there was a costly withdrawal in August of 2022. The United States managed to save some Afghan people from the brutality of the Taliban. Unfortunately, this effort is largely overshadowed by the countless Afghans left behind who once were hopeful that the United States would establish a new democratic government in Afghanistan. Many Afghans who worked with the coalition forces were killed, or targeted for killing, during and after the Taliban takeover in August of 2021.

The United States spent years attempting to train and arm the new Afghan military to prevent it from falling to the Taliban and\or ISIS when the American troops withdrew to go home. The withdrawal was a complete failure. After two years of negotiations with the Taliban in Doha, Qatar, the United States, under President Joseph Biden, decided that 20 years of fighting was enough and the American troops were to be sent home by September 11, 2021, on the 20 year anniversary of the September 11th attacks. During the summer of 2021, this date was moved to August 31, 2021. As the American troops began withdrawing from multiple provincial capitals in Afghanistan, the Taliban quickly re-took these capitals within a span of two weeks, gaining ammunition and vehicles from the Afghan soldiers the US-trained and supplied, and releasing prisoners to join their ranks.

In Aug. of 2021, the American CIA began warning President Biden that the capital of Afghanistan, Kabul, would fall within one month if the US continued its withdrawal of troops. President Joseph Biden decided to continue the withdrawal and Kabul fell two days later. Fearing for his safety, Afghan President Ashraf Ghani fled to the United Arab Emirates. Kabul was overrun and personnel and staff at the American Embassy, the Australian Embassy, the Canadian embassy, and several European embassies began shredding documents, disposing of American flags, and evacuating for an immediate withdrawal from Afghanistan.

Thousands of citizens in Afghanistan have helped the US over the years to fight the Taliban in various ways including spying and translating. Others worked for women's rights, assuring that females received education and job opportunities over the past 20 years. Many of these citizens fear for their lives under Taliban control. Several of them were issued American visas and were allowed to travel out of the country before the final takeover of Afghanistan by the Taliban.

In August of 2021, thousands of Afghans flocked to the airport to try to escape from Afghanistan with their lives due to several different rumors that there was a possibility that they would be allowed evacuation before the final withdrawal of American troops. On August 16, 2021, all commercial flights were "canceled as five people were reportedly killed at the airport as people scrambled to leave Afghanistan" (Al Jazeera). The stampede at the airport caused parents to pass their babies over an airport wall to American military personnel in an attempt to keep the babies from being trampled to death. Sohail Ahmadi, a two month old baby at the time, was "handed in desperation to a soldier across an airport wall" (Al Jazeera). He was separated from his family for almost five months. Several people died while trying to cling to a military plane that was evacuating Afghanistan. One individual who died this way was Zaki Anwari, a 17-year-old member of Afghanistan's National Youth Soccer team (Fassihi). A second person was Fada Mohammed, a young dentist who fled for the airport without informing any of his family members that he was trying to escape (Shih). Many Afghan citizens that helped the United States remain trapped in Afghanistan and are terrified for their lives.

As of January of 2022, an estimated 100 people have been killed by the Taliban since the US withdrawal, most likely as retribution for siding with the US. This happened, despite the Taliban's many promises that there would be no retribution and all was forgiven. Also, during the fall of 2021, there were long lines at ATMs, and people were not allowed to withdraw more than $200 per week. The winter of 2022 has left 95% of Afghans on the brink of starvation.

The new Taliban government needs to establish itself and its ability to collect taxes and fees at checkpoints. It also needs to provide goods and services. The Taliban claims it is turning over a new leaf. The group promised that they would no longer be selling opium or discriminating against women. Five months on and only women whose jobs cannot be done by men are allowed in the workplace. Few schools have read-mitted girls since the takeover. The international community is refusing to acknowledge the Taliban and is restricting aid to the starving in Afghanistan because there is no trust that money sent into a Taliban-controlled country will be used for humanitarian needs.

The swarm of violence during August of 2021's Taliban takeover only created more homeless. As the winter of 2022 sets in, many Afghans are likely to starve to death.

It was my honor to interview a female special forces fighter from Afghanistan who participated in over 500 missions against the Taliban. She, and her husband Mohammad, now call the United States their home.

MALIKA AND MOHAMMAD'S STORY

Malika is 35 years old; her husband is 37. They both grew up in the Kandahar region of Afghanistan. As children, they entertained themselves by playing cricket, soccer, and tag with their siblings and friends.

When Russia withdrew from Afghanistan in 1996, they were 11 and nine years old. The Taliban filled the power vacuum left behind by Russia and became the controlling government. Mohammad and Malika lived under strict and oppressive Taliban control. The Taliban intimidated girls and women, preventing them from attending school and holding occupations. One tactic used regularly by the Taliban was throwing acid on the faces of girls walking home from school. They also attacked the teachers and burned schools down to oppress women and keep them at home.

Malika is the second wife of Mohammad. He and his ex-wife divorced several years ago. Mohammad and Malika met when they were both in their 30s; they were working for an international humanitarian organization. They decided to get married in 2020.

Malika was a military sergeant in the Afghan special forces. She was involved in over 500 missions in collaboration with the coalition forces against the Taliban and ISIS. When the United States began its withdrawal from Afghanistan in the

summer of 2021, Malika and Mohammad knew that they were in a very dangerous situation. Malika is wanted by the Taliban for working with the United States.

For their safety, Mohammad and Malika needed to flee Kandahar when the Taliban took over Afghanistan in the summer of 2021. They fled their home in Kandahar for Kabul airport. They were unable to get onto a flight due to the swarm of Afghans attempting to escape the Taliban. Malika contacted her US military colonel who was stationed at the Pentagon. From her station at the Pentagon, Malika's colonel was finally able to remove Malika, her husband, and one of her stepsons from Afghanistan, in October of 2022.

Mohammad has three sons from a previous marriage. They were only able to bring his 14-year-old son with them to America. His other two sons are 16 and six years old. They remain in Afghanistan with their mother.

Mohammad and Malika are truly grateful that they were able to move to the United States and escape the Taliban with their lives. However, they miss their families very much.

I interviewed Mohammad and Malika on February 19, 2022. Mohammad translated for his wife. She does not speak English.

PART ONE

VOCAB

Taliban: An "ultraconservative political and religious faction that emerged in Afghanistan in the mid-1990s following the withdrawal of Soviet troops, the collapse of Afghanistan's communist regime, and the subsequent breakdown in civil order" (Britannica). The Taliban is known for suppressing women's rights and human rights.

Talib: A member of the Taliban.

Coalition forces in Afghanistan: Several nations that took on Al-Qaeda and the Taliban during Operation Enduring Freedom in Afghanistan.

GUIDING QUESTION

What type of person comes to mind when you think of someone who fought the Taliban?

"How did the American invasion of Afghanistan and the 20 years of war affect you personally?" I asked.

"I was only 17 years old when the American invasion happened. My wife was 15. We were students attempting to get an education. We were excited that the United States was invading. We were expecting that we were going to get new freedoms, the types of freedoms that we hear that Americans have such as the ability for girls to go to school and hold jobs.

We supported the United States against the Taliban. Malika's father was a chief military commander who fought alongside the Americans. He was killed by the Taliban for siding with the coalition forces. Some Taliban members noticed him shopping in the marketplace in 2017. They walked up to him and shot him in the head. This inspired Malika to sign up to be in the special forces, to fight against the Taliban, and to protect human beings and their freedoms in Afghanistan.

Malika was involved in over 500 operations against the Taliban and ISIS. She was engaged in joint operations with the coalition forces. In many of the operations, she was the only woman. The culture in Afghanistan is that no one can enter someone else's home without permission. As the only female in the unit, it was her job to go into homes first and request permission to enter. This was very risky because she was often the first soldier entering the homes of Taliban and ISIS fighters.

Malika engaged in several operations per night, usually starting at midnight. She jumped out of helicopters roughly four or six km away from her targets. The coordinates were given to her unit by the coalition forces. She and the other soldiers pursued the Taliban on foot under the cover of darkness. The missions included retrieving information, removing weapons, capturing insurgents, and attacking them. Her unit tried to succeed at its missions without engaging in violence. Unfortunately, this was often impossible. Malika and the Afghan forces were the boots on the ground. The coalition forces were the reinforcements in the sky. After Malika's unit completed its operations by taking targeted areas from Taliban control, the coalition forces might join them on the ground. Usually, they remained in the air, keeping the air space clear. Malika worked a 24 hour day; and then she would be allowed 24 hours to rest at home.

Her most heartbreaking experiences were those which involved children. On one particular mission, she was informed that there was a large number of explosives being kept by a Talib commander in his home. This Talib was preparing roadside bombs inside his home, near his family members, putting their lives at risk. Handmade bombs are extremely dangerous. Malika and her unit could not safely remove the explosives from the home; the house needed to be entirely destroyed. Upon her arrival at the home, the Talib fighter escaped; but he left his family behind.

When Malika entered the home she encountered the Talib fighter's wife, his three children, and an elderly woman. They were completely terrified of her. She decided to hug the family members and tell them that she was there to protect them from the dangerous explosive devices in their home. The children were shaking in her arms. She comforted the family as best she could. She said 'we are here to save your lives; we are sisters. We won't hurt you! We are here to rescue you.' She took two of the children in her arms and put the elderly woman on her back. The third child and the wife walked out with them. Once she removed the family safely from the home, the next step was to remove all of the neighbors from their homes as well. When the area was clear of people, they sent word to the American coalition forces above to explode the home, thereby destroying the explosive devices inside.

Malika asked the people they removed from the neighborhood if they had any relatives in other villages that they could go stay with now that they were homeless. The ones who did stayed with their family members. If not, Malika connected them with people in other villages that took them in for a night. Following the one-night stay, Malika's unit connected them with UNICEF for assistance with housing.

Malika received The *"Symbol of Honor for National Police"* in Afghanistan for her bravery and her efforts.

One example of her bravery was a mission in Helmand province in 2021. She, and 40 of her fellow soldiers, jumped from the coalition helicopter and traveled on foot to their target, a

Malika's "Symbol of Honor for National Police" in Afghanistan

group of what they were told was 15 Taliban fighters. The coordinates were about 15 km from the jump. Her commander led the unit, bravely walking in front of the group. Unfortunately, when they came upon the Taliban, they realized that their intel was wrong. It was not a group of 15 Taliban in the area. Instead, there were over 100 Taliban in the area.

Upon encountering the Taliban, her commander was shot in the stomach. He was trapped and there was no one to take command of the unit. Malika decided to take charge herself. She was determined to save her commander. She contacted headquarters via her walkie-talkie, informing them that they were outnumbered and the commander was injured and separated from the rest of her unit. He was alone, bleeding heavily, lying down, and coming under fire from the Taliban fighters who were about 50m away.

She decided to take matters into her own hands. She went into the villages and removed three of the local civilians who supported the Taliban. She, and two other soldiers, used them as human shields. They walked behind the civilians, with their guns to the shoulders of the civilians, to enter enemy lines and rescue her commander. The Taliban stopped shooting because they did not want to injure their own villagers. She was able to remove her commander by pulling him to safety. Although it only took Malika 40 minutes to successfully remove her commander, he died shortly after his removal to the helicopter.

Once Malika's force was off the ground and safe in the sky, they gave the coordinates of the Taliban to the coalition forces. The entire area was bombarded."

GUIDING QUESTION

What type of person comes to mind when you think of someone who fought the Taliban?

PART TWO

VOCAB
Withdrawal from Afghanistan: After 20 years of fighting in Afghanistan, the Biden administration pulled all US servicemen out of Afghanistan in August of 2021. This ended the stalemate with the Taliban and allowed the Taliban to quickly take back total control of the country.

GUIDING QUESTION
Why is it important to understand the experiences of others?

"What experiences did you have surrounding the American withdrawal from Afghanistan?"

"When the Taliban took over our country this summer we lost everything. We fled our home in Kandahar, running for our lives. Now that we are settled here in the US, we get updates from our friends and family back home about the Taliban. Recently, my friend sent me a photo of Taliban members living in my home. They just took it over.

Luckily, Malika's American colonel acted as our sponsor to get us out of Afghanistan with our lives. Malika received a letter in June of 2021 from the Taliban. It stated that the Taliban was looking for her and that they were intending to murder her. Malika emailed her colonel informing her that the country was in a very serious downward spiral and that we needed help.

By August of 2021, Malika's colonel advised us to get to Kabul airport and get on a flight for the United States. She said this was the only way to save our lives. We knew this was true because as the Taliban was taking over Kandahar we saw the

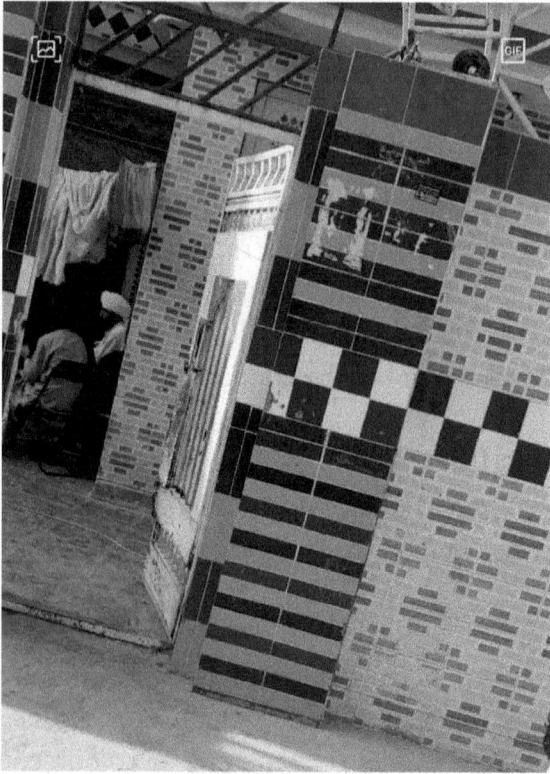

Taliban who moved themselves into Malika and Mohammad's home.

local people who had stood against the Taliban murdered in the streets. The dead bodies were just left behind. When Malika first saw this happen she called the police captain and argued that they should fight against the Taliban and not fear them. But even the police were too afraid of the Taliban's strength without the Americans to back them up. To compound this, Afghanistan's President Ashraf Ghani fled the country, and with the Americans withdrawing as well, everyone else was giving up. Of course, the local police quit their positions.

We realized that there was no hope. Malika went home and burned all documents relating to her identity to prevent the Taliban from arresting her or her family members. Unfortunately, Malika has many enemies in Afghanistan who are continuing to look for her because she fought against the Taliban. Now that she has fled Afghanistan, Taliban members still regularly check her relatives' and friends' homes searching for her.

The gripping fear of the murderous Taliban is the reason why thousands of Afghans swarmed Kabul airport in August of 2021. This is why people tried to hold onto airplanes as they were taking off. This is why there was a swarm of people panicking to the point where babies had to be passed over airport walls to American military officials, saving them from being trampled in the stampede.

Unfortunately, when we arrived at Kabul airport it was blocked off. One day before, there was a terrorist attack by ISIS-K at the airport. 13 American servicemen were killed along with 60 Afghan civilians. 140 Afghans were wounded. This made the already chaotic situation even more tragic and stressful.

Malika's colonel continued to try to assist us from the Pentagon. She was also assisting 13 other military families from Afghanistan that she had worked with. We traveled together with the other families on a large bus to another province of Afghanistan, Mazar. We were housed there temporarily in a hotel that belonged to the UN. The hotel was secure, but Mazar was under Taliban control; the situation was very tenuous. We were there for 20 days and then they assisted us with applying to Qatar for removal from Afghanistan.

We stayed at the US Marine base in Qatar. The service people there gave us all the vaccinations we needed before we could enter the United States, including the COVID vaccine. Then we boarded a flight for Virginia. We stayed in a refugee camp in Virginia for a month and a half.

Luckily, we moved to Rhode Island. We were able to move here because we have family here. My cousin has been living in Rhode Island for almost five years now. He told us if we moved here he would help us to adjust to the American way of life. Also, Providence is a quiet city. My wife is tired from all of the fighting in Afghanistan. She just wants to live a quiet life now. We love it here in Rhode Island. It is a very nice place.

We are working in a jewelry factory in Lincoln. We send any extra money that we have home to Afghanistan. This is because the economic situation is dire. Our friends and family at home in Afghanistan are on the brink of starvation.

Malika is very happy to be here in the United States. But she still worries about her brothers. One of her brothers fought against the Taliban as well. In August of 2022, he was shot in the foot during a firefight with the Taliban. Her other brother works for human rights. Now, they are both in hiding; they live in constant fear of being killed by the Taliban. We applied to have Malika's two brothers removed from Afghanistan, but it was denied because her brothers never worked directly with the Americans.

We can never return home to Afghanistan because if we do we will put our lives at risk. The situation there is very tenuous. Women have no rights. Girls cannot go to school. Women who used to be able to be part of the workforce are now forced to stay home.

The Taliban is acting more reasonably in the big cities such as Kabul. This is because they are trying to have a decent reputation with the rest of the globe. But outside of the major cities, they are engaging in brutal punishments such as cutting off a person's hand for stealing. But this is not reported in the media because the Taliban does not allow the media to take any reports about their activities. There is rhetoric that the Taliban has changed, that the Taliban will be better than it was in the 90s and that the Taliban may even allow women to have rights. However, you cannot trust the Taliban. They are not a group that can be trusted. The United Nations needs to step in and do something about the human rights violations in Afghanistan."

"Malika, what is one message that you have for American students?" I asked.

"I worked for my country as a policewoman and as a soldier. But I fight for all humans and for human dignity. No religion, ethnicity or language should divide us. We are all human beings. We should be one family."

GUIDING QUESTION

Why is it important to understand the experiences of others?

BACKGROUND ON SEPT. IITH FOR STUDENTS AND TEACHERS

Why was the United States at war with Afghanistan for 20 years?

The tragic events of September 11th will forever shape the American landscape. On September 11, 2001, four American passenger planes were hijacked. The mastermind behind the attacks was Osama bin Laden. He planned the attacks from his base in Afghanistan; 15 of the hijackers were from Saudi Arabia, two were from the United Arab Emirates, one was from Lebanon and one was from Egypt. One plane was flown into each of the Twin Towers in New York City. A third plane was flown into the Pentagon. The final plane, *Flight 93*, was overtaken by the passengers and crashed in Shanksville, Pennsylvania.

2,996 people died including:

- 246 people on four planes
- 2,606 people in New York City

- 125 at the Pentagon
- 411 emergency workers
- 55 military personnel"*

Additionally, many survivors and first responders who came to help were exposed to noxious dust, chemicals and fumes that have caused illness and death. "Researchers have identified more than 60 types of cancer and about two dozen other conditions that are linked to Ground Zero exposures. As of today, at least 4,627 responders and survivors enrolled in the World Trade Center (WTC) Health Program have died" (Haelle). Thousands of others continue to suffer from severe health conditions caused by exposures at Ground Zero.

US citizens were furious that their American brethren, who woke up and went to work on a Tuesday morning in September, were brutally murdered in a surprise terrorist attack in the United States. The president at the time, George W. Bush, visited the wreckage of the World Trade Center Towers and made the emotional statement that "the people who knocked these buildings down will hear all of us soon" (fox29.com). The American mantra became we will "never forget" and the desire for revenge grew into a fury (WCTV.tv).

"On October 7, 2001, a U.S. led coalition began attacks on Taliban-controlled Afghanistan with an intense bombing campaign by American and British forces" (history.com). The war in Afghanistan lasted for 20 brutal years.

---

*   September 11—102 minutes that shocked the world part three documentary

THE HUMAN COST*

- American service members killed in Afghanistan through April: 2,448.
- U.S. contractors: 3,846
- Afghan national military and police: 66,000
- Other allied service members, including from other NATO member states: 1,144
- Afghan civilians: 47,245
- Taliban and other opposition fighters: 51,191
- Aid workers: 444
- Journalists: 72

Why was Afghanistan blamed for the Sept. 11th attacks? One cause is the very existence of the Taliban. The Taliban is a fundamentalist Islamic group that took over Afghanistan in 1996 when the Soviet Union withdrew from Afghanistan. The Taliban follows a strict version of Sharia Law. In the 1990s, for example, under Taliban control, women in Afghanistan were not allowed to work, they followed a strict dress code including covering their faces, and were not allowed to travel without a male companion. The Taliban quickly became known for its brutality.

The second reason is Osama bin Laden. The Taliban offered a safe haven to Osama bin Laden who fought as a member of the mujahideen against the Soviet Union in Afghanistan during the Cold War. Many mujahideen later became Taliban. Osama bin Laden was already exiled from his home country of Saudi Arabia and few countries would take him in because of his ties to international terrorism. Osama bin Laden staged other previous terrorist attacks against the United States including the

---

*   Knickmeyer

attack on the American embassies in Tanzania and Kenya. The Taliban allowed Osama bin Laden to live in Afghanistan under the condition that he did not attack other nations. Instead, he chose to create a terrorist network in Afghanistan known as Al Qaeda and plan the deadliest terrorist attack in American history. The US blamed Osama bin Laden, Al Qaeda, and, in turn, the Taliban for the September 11th attacks. The Taliban denied Osama bin Laden's involvement.

Osama bin Laden had several grievances with the United States. Firstly, he was angry with the United States for aiding and supporting Israel more than the Palestinians in their dispute over Israel. Secondly, he was angry that the United States led the UN in maintaining sanctions placed on Iraq because Saddam Hussein refused to meet all requirements to disarm his weapons. This caused severe economic hardships for the people of Iraq. Thirdly, he viewed it as wrong for there to be an American military base stationed on what he considered to be sacred Muslim land in Saudi Arabia.

Even though Osama bin Laden was Saudi Arabian, the United States decided to attack Afghanistan, his current home. The goals of the invasion of Afghanistan were the assassination of Osama bin Laden, the destruction of Al-Qaeda, his terrorist network, and the removal of the Taliban from power. Osama bin Laden hid in the Hindu Kush mountains, evading capture for almost a decade.

Osama bin Laden was finally captured and killed in Pakistan on May 2 of 2011. The Taliban was removed from power but managed to continue to control the mountainous regions of Afghanistan, often ambushing American soldiers along the few paved roads in Afghanistan. After 18 years of fighting, the United States and the Afghan military it trained remained in a stalemate with the Taliban and began to negotiate a peaceful withdrawal from Afghanistan under the Trump administration.

The US was hoping to keep the Afghan military and government of President Ashraf Ghani in place after the withdrawal, though many doubted the new Afghan military could hold out against the Taliban without the support of the US.

A NOTE TO TEACHERS

After finishing the discussion questions in this reading, I recommend that you reach out to NaTakallam for a cultural interaction with a refugee from Afghanistan. Offer students the opportunity to act as journalists by creating unique and culturally sensitive questions to ask during the interview. Make sure to inform NaTakallam that you read this chapter from *Refugee Realities.*

This is the link: https://natakallam.com/education/

PRINTABLE WORKSHEET FOR STUDENTS

	Answer the Guiding Question below before reading each section.	Answer the Guiding Question below after reading each section. Use a specific quote from the text to back up your thinking.
What type of person comes to mind when you think of someone who fought the Taliban?		
Why is it important to understand the experiences of others?		

CHAPTER FOUR

AN INTERVIEW WITH LAYLA
SYRIAN WOMAN WHO IS NOW A REFUGEE IN TURKEY

In Syria, in February of 2011, three boys were arrested in the city of Deraa for allegedly painting graffiti that spoke poorly of the Syrian dictator Bashar al-Assad. When their parents asked government officials at the political security chief's office where their children were, the government official's response was extremely offensive. The parents were told "forget your children. If you want children, make more children. If you don't know how, bring us your women and we will make them for you" (Malek 167).

This outraged the Syrian population and "led by the boys' fathers, protesters soon took to the streets of Deraa" (Lemmon 33). When the boys were finally released, they were so badly beaten they were almost unrecognizable. Their teeth were missing and their limbs were broken. Thousands upon thousands took to the streets not only because of this outrage, but because of many incidences of brutality and corruption by the Assad regime.

For example, in Syria if you earn a degree from a university you can't simply apply for a job. You have to bribe your employer in order to get your job. Frequently, people who do not even hold certificates receive jobs that they are not trained for because they bribed their way into their positions. It may take a university graduate anywhere from six to ten years to save up enough money for the bribe to get a decent paying job. Further, if a Syrian needs anything from the government, such as a national identification card, the Syrian usually needs to first manage to gather together the money to bribe the government officials.

Furthermore, an estimated 1.6 million to 2.5 million Syrians are actually of Kurdish descent. However, they are not allowed to speak the Kurdish language, dress in Kurdish style clothes, dance or sing Kurdish style dances, watch anything Kurdish on television, "travel abroad, own property, or take university slots because the regime had long denied them national identification cards" (Lemmon 34). If they do manage to engage in any of these activities they are often arrested. This is because the Kurds do not have their own nation and Bashar al-Assad is afraid that if the Kurds have many liberties, and can embrace their own unique culture, they may also pursue and succeed at the founding of their own nation in northeast Syria, which would ultimately mean the loss of some of Assad's territory.

In 2011 the Syrians took to protesting in the streets in hope of a better country. What happened next is shocking!

PART ONE

VOCAB

Arab Spring: "The Arab Spring was a movement in favor of democracy in the Arab world. The movement began in Tunisia in 2010. It soon spread to other countries in North Africa and the Middle East" such as Morocco, Syria, Libya, Egypt and Bahrain (Kids Britannica). Many people joined the movement because they believed their governments were unfair and dishonest. Several of the countries that rebelled had corrupt rulers who had created economic situations that were untenable. The people who rebelled were hoping for a better government, and, in turn, a better life. In the end, the gravity of the destruction and death caused by the Syrian uprising was dire.

GUIDING QUESTION

Why is freedom of the press important?

LAYLA'S STORY

Layla is a lovely Syrian woman who is about to turn 30 years old. She has long dark hair, high cheekbones, large piercing eyes and a contagious smile. She does not cover her hair. When she was 19 years old her country spiraled into a civil war. She was caught in the middle of the trauma, tumult and catastrophe that followed. She attended several protests against the regime of Bashar al Assad but eventually, after being arrested and assaulted several times, she decided to flee her home country of Syria for Istanbul, Turkey. She lives there with her husband and her two sons; but she longs for the family she left behind in Syria. She wonders regularly if she will ever see her parents or her cousins again.

Layla is very approachable. She is easy to talk to but clearly has a maturity about her that is beyond her years. She has endured severe trauma and she is not afraid to talk about it. In fact, she wants her story to be heard. She hopes for a better future for the Syrian people.

I interviewed Layla on March 14, 2021.

We met via Zoom. She was in Istanbul, Turkey. I was in the United States. I started by asking about her background. "What was your life like in Syria before the Civil War began?", I asked.

"I come from a small town, so our life was simple. We would visit our relatives and friends or socialize at cafes. We had only one large park we frequented and a few smaller ones. We also visited the mountains when the weather was beautiful to spend some time together and have family adventures. We loved to venture out to the citadel near our home.

I was a student at a hotel training institute. Later, during the war, I applied again to earn my high school diploma with slightly better grades and I started to study English literature," she explained.

"It appears that your life was quite nice before the Syrian Civil War. What were the main reasons the protests started happening where you lived in Syria?", I asked.

"Well, we were a bit inspired. The Arab Spring began in other countries, and people in Syria at first were scared but hoped that perhaps the Syrians could request some changes from the government. So, allegedly, a bunch of kids wrote some graffiti. For example, they wrote 'Your Turn is Coming Doctor' because Bashar al Assad used to be an eye doctor. They also wrote 'The People Want to Overthrow the Regime'. The kids were arrested and tortured. Their fingers were broken and they suffered torture by electric shock. That was the spark; people started to protest. They demanded that the government employees who tortured the boys would be held responsible.

But the government did nothing, after a short while Bashar al Assad delivered a speech on the TV but didn't mention anything about the boys or the protests. Instead, he spoke vaguely about a conspiracy against Syria led by other countries. That's what made people start to demand Bashar al Assad's resignation. They wanted to change the entire government.

But Syrian national TV channels lied from the beginning. They said no protests were happening. If they did mention a protest on TV they stated that it was very small in number. And we heard so many rumors. For example, the TV channels claimed that the people who protested were paid to do so or drug addicts, among other rumors. The TV channels were trying to portray that it was not a real people's revolution."

GUIDING QUESTION

How could this situation have gone differently if there was freedom of the press in Syria?

PART TWO

VOCAB
Damascus: The capital of Syria.

GUIDING QUESTION
Why is freedom of speech and the right to peacefully protest important?

"How terrible it truly is when the media lies to the general public," I responded. "You must have been very angry if you understood what was happening. Have you ever been to, or participated in, a protest against Assad?"

She responded with a serious expression. "I've participated in almost every protest I could because we heard about the revolutions happening in other countries. We believed that we could change our country for the better, even if Assad didn't leave, we believed we could at least change some things in the country.

Unfortunately, everything became worse. Arresting people began and there were so many stories of torture and missing people. These incidents made people protest more and more. Unfortunately, the response was not as we expected. The government became more brutal in some cities."

"I have heard the stories of the brutality of the Syrian regime against the protesters. Were you ever arrested?", I asked.

"I participated in a protest in Damascus. The main slogan for that protest was 'Stop the Blood; Stop the Killings'. It was in front of the Parliament building. Unfortunately, they started to arrest and beat people in the street.

I was arrested with my friend and several men and women.

They took the men first and kept the women in the car waiting. After a few minutes, they took us as well. When we entered we saw all the men laying on the floor all bloody and most of them were unconscious, or pretending to be unconscious, so that the beating would stop.

They lined up the women and started to beat us with a thick stick. They sexually harassed us and threatened us that if we spent the night we would be physically and sexually assaulted.

Then we were taken to be interrogated. They asked if we participated in the protest. Surely, most of us lied and pretended to be just passing by.

But two women were known to them as being arrested before.

They released most of us but kept the two women and I've never heard about them after that. I'm not sure if they were ever released or if they died in prison, which is common in Syria.

The men were all kept there overnight. I don't know what happened to them; but one of my male friends got out after a month and a half. He had been tortured and he was very skinny.

Most men won't say for sure what happened in prison but we can guess. However, sometimes it is obvious. Some released prisoners had visible scars from cigarettes on their bodies, or their hair and/or nails, or more, had been removed."

"Clearly, it was very dangerous for you to protest in Syria. What inspired you to risk bodily harm, and possibly death, to protest anyway?" I asked.

"It is very complicated to describe. There is so much that is astonishingly unfair in Syria. For example, in Syria, emergency laws exist so they can arrest any Syrian without charges. The person arrested could simply disappear and you can't do anything about it. They can just take a person and say he was suspected of doing something related to terrorism, or against the government, and there is no need for proof. Arrested Syrians do not have the right to one phone call. So their family members don't even know what prison they were taken to, or if they were arrested at all. The arrested people just disappear.

Also, people regularly frame each other in Syria. They are commonly referred to as 'rats.' Corruption is everywhere, even if a person did a violent crime, if this person knows someone in a high place, or pays enough money, the person will get away with it.

If you applied for a job and someone is more connected than you, the connected person will get the job. For me, it was very difficult to get a job in Syria. Most of my friends that were able to get teaching jobs had to pay someone to arrange a job for them. Or they had to arrange a 'special relationship' with a man in order to get a job.

In Syria they also monopolized the national economy, whereby all private companies located in Syria are affiliated with relatives of the regime, such as telecommunications, textile and others. Officials in government departments are usually subordinate to relatives of the president's family. Courts are full of financial and administrative corruption. So if you have a court case of any kind, and your opponent is more connected, you will lose. Even for small commercial enterprises, if there is a competitor to the regime, the project would not continue due to the pressures of the authority in terms of sending violations and delaying commercial transactions. These are just some of the many reasons I decided to risk my life to protest in Syria.

GUIDING QUESTION

Why is freedom of speech and the right to peacefully protest important? How might the situations in Syria have gone differently if the people had these rights?

PART THREE

VOCAB

Alwai: "A follower of 'Ali,' the Prophet Muhammad's cousin and son-in-law. The 'Alawis (and all Shia Muslims) believe that 'Ali was Muhammad's rightful heir to the political and spiritual leadership of the Muslim community" (Encyclopedia.com).

Palestine: "The geographic region located between the Mediterranean Sea and the Jordan River. Today, Palestine theoretically includes the West Bank (a territory that sits between modern-day Israel and Jordan) and the Gaza Strip (which borders modern-day Israel and Egypt)" (history.com). Most Palestinian Muslims, as well as many people of other religions and ethnicities, believe Palestinian land was stolen from them by the Jewish refugees who fled World War II and settled in the newly created nation of Israel.

Islam's Army: A fundamentalist Islamic unit that is anti-Assad and pro Sharia Law. Unfortunately, Sharia Law is often misinterpreted by different ideologies, sometimes for political purposes. Islam's Army is supported by Saudi Arabia and one of its goals is to create an Islamic State.

Salafist: "The Salafi-jihadi ideology, which has existed in its current form since at least the 1960s and holds that it is the duty of every true Muslim to use force to reestablish a caliphate as it existed in the early years of Islam" (criticalthreats.org).

Ahrar al Sham: "A Sunni Salafist militant group operating in Syria that aims to replace the Assad Regime with an Islamic government" (stanford.edu).

Al Qaeda: The terrorist organization responsible for Sept. 11th.

Jihadist: "An Islamic fundamentalist who participates in, or supports, jihad, especially armed and violent confrontation" (dictionary.com).

GUIDING QUESTION
Why would an evil dictator want to portray himself as good to the international community?

"Layla, why is it that Assad is so popular with some people in Syria, considering all of the corruption in the Syrian government?" I asked.

"In Syria, there are so many religious sects. The majority, about 80%, are Sunni. The rest are a combination of many other minorities. One of the minorities is the "Alawi". Around 10% of the Syrians are Alawi. So this sect, most of them, are supporters of Assad because they believe if he is gone then they will be gone too. They fear they will lose their positions and also they fear death because they were terrible to the rest of the people. So they fear revenge if Assad loses power. The Alawi portrayed themselves as the protectors of all minorities, and even the entire Syrian population, from 'extremists'. So a lot of people fear the change of the regime because they are fearful of terrorists.

This is why most Syrian people believe that Bashar al Assad was actually responsible for founding ISIS. Some of Assad's opponents believe he was involved in founding ISIS, but there is no proof. The theory is that Assad created the monster, ISIS, for the people to fear. If the people were preoccupied with being afraid of ISIS they would be more likely to support Assad as a better option than the alternative. For example, on the borders of Damascus, where I grew up, many extremists were trying to enter through the borders of my city. This terrified people. Due to this fear, a large number of Syrian citizens joined the mercenaries to protect their city from ISIS. This benefitted the regime. So people eventually had one of two really bad choices.

Also, a lot of Syrians watch only the national TV channel and believe whatever they broadcast. So they believe that the regime is actually not bad, just a lonely wolf."

"That is unfortunate," I responded. "By a lonely wolf do you mean that other countries don't support Assad?"

"Yes, exactly, and the regime keeps talking about Palestine and how we, as Arabs, should stick together. The regime keeps talking about unity so people tend to feel they should stand with the government because it has a good case especially against ISIS and Israel.

We hear stories that exist on the internet also. We have heard that the Syrian prisons held 'extremists' who were released after the revolution began. Most of them moved to different cities and they established factions. One example is Zahran Alloush. He was released in 2012, less than one year after the Syrian Civil War began. After that, he founded Islam's Army in 2013, also known as Jaysh al-Islam. It was one of the biggest factions of the time. Releasing a rebellious extremist such as Zahran Alloush during a civil war doesn't make sense. Why was the Syrian government releasing rebellious extremists during a civil war, but not innocent protesters? It was as if Assad was purposely creating more chaos so he could act as the hero who fixed the problem to the world.

Another example is Hassan Abboud. He was in the regime's prisons since 2004 and was released several months after the beginning of the revolution. He is a hard line Salafist extremist who founded the Ahrar al-Sham faction at the end of 2011, and was killed by a mysterious bombing in 2014.

Another example is Hassan Soufan who was studying in Saudi Arabia. The Saudi government gave him up to the Syrian regime who kept him prisoner for 12 years in Syria. He was released in 2016, during the civil war, and he became the leader of the Ahrar al Sham faction.

Do you get the idea? Assad was releasing extremists who would cause more chaos so that he could look like the better option to the Syrians and the global community. Think about it, even the US helped Assad fight ISIS because the situation was so dire.

Most of these factions began as a branch of the Free Army but after a while, they got separated and became more extreme and then arrested people and tortured people exactly as the regime did. They arrested people with no specific reason or evidence. Anyone who criticized them, or stood against them, just like the regime, was arrested and often tortured. The Free Syrian Army was established to free Syria from the brutal regime of Bashar al-Assad. But the Free Syrian Army actually created prisons that were arguably scarier than the regime's prisons."

I responded to her. "Ah, I see. Assad kept many of his sup-porters because the alternatives were often worse! Wasn't it a handful of Syrian army officers who 'defected and created the opposition Free Syrian army'? (Lemmon 34). I thought this was supposed to be better than the regime."

"Unfortunately, it did not turn out that way! In fact, in 2012, the leader of Al Qaeda spoke out against Assad. This caused jihadists to see Syria as good real estate for them," Layla responded.

"So it started to become more and more obvious that the alternatives to Assad were not necessarily better" I said.

"Sadly, yes," she answered.

GUIDING QUESTION

Layla believes that Assad released prisoners in his own country to cause havoc. If this is true, what was he hoping to get from the international community by doing this?

PART FOUR

VOCAB

Habeas Corpus: "A writ requiring a person under arrest to be brought before a judge or into court, especially to secure the person's release unless lawful grounds are shown for their detention" (Oxford languages). This is a right Americans have in the United States. It essentially means that Americans cannot be sent to prison without just cause.

GUIDING QUESTION

Why is habeas corpus an important right?

"Layla, what, would you argue, is the actual percentage of people who truly support Bashar al Assad?"

"That question is very complicated to answer, very complicated. Most of the people in Syria now are too poor or too scared to think of anything related to the revolution. The regime is making their lives now very difficult because of the high prices of goods and inflation which caused the value of the Syrian pound to fall. Life is very hard. Most people enlist in the army, or special forces, just to get paid so they can manage to live. Also, the regime gives their soldiers more power by providing them with guns so that they can rob and do whatever helps them to survive. Enlisted soldiers are likely to get away with any crime they commit, especially against a person who is not connected. So no one actually knows the percentage of people who support Assad. But we think most people just don't dare to talk about it if they don't support him."

"It sounds as if connected people in Syria regularly get away with crimes. Have you ever witnessed human rights violations happening?" I asked.

"Well of course there was the horrible experience I had when I was arrested. I was threatened and beaten. Also, when I saw my friends get arrested, and saw the marks on their bodies, it was very sad. For example, the last time my brother was arrested he stayed in prison for a month. He endured a lot of permanent damage to his wrists. In Syrian prisons there is what we call 'shabh'. This is when they put ropes on prisoners' hands and then hang them from their hands. So it damages the wrists and the shoulders; the longer they do it the more damage it causes.

I also saw cigarette marks on my friends' bodies. My cousin stayed in jail for almost two months. He was sexually harassed and his hair was cut off, bit by bit.

Also, the regime security forces used to beat us when they came to any protest. It became normal to get beaten up. Once I was going to protest in Damascus in a very famous place, al Midan. Every week in that place people were killed for protesting. The following week they would hold another protest and more people would be killed. Even when they took the bodies to bury the security forces came and shot the people burying the bodies. They also shot bystanders. This went on week after week.

But when I went there, luckily for me, the protest was canceled because security forces were there before us.

One of the people I know was arrested and his back was injured from being tortured. It was all marked with what appeared to be knife marks. The regime suspected that he had joined the Free Syria Army which is anti-Assad. After a while he was found murdered, alone at his farm. Other farmers said they saw security forces come and that they just started shooting at him; they didn't want to arrest him. They wanted him dead. He was only 22 years old.

Once in Hama, we organized a protest for only women. We protested to ask for the detainees to be released from prison. There were almost 30 of us. Then the security forces came in their cars. Some women ran and about 15 of us stayed. They started to beat us up and kicked us out, literally.

Also, once a friend of mine was killed at a protest in Damascus. We went to bury him but while doing so we held signs for freedom and stuff like that. The graveyard we were going to is outside the city; it is near the mountains. In the mountains there was a new military base. The soldiers started shooting at people. At first, they were shooting above people just to intimidate us. Shortly thereafter they started shooting directly at people. No one knows exactly how many people were injured because no one dared to go to the hospital for fear of arrest. A good friend of mine was shot in the leg; he survived. One person died on that day. He was shot but no one was able to help him because they were shooting randomly. So he was drained of blood and eventually died. Later in the evening, the military base allowed an ambulance to go get his body and search to see if anyone else was still stuck out there."

"I am so sorry for everything you went through and everything you have seen", I explained with a look of sincere empathy. "I understand that people often protest in Syria because of the thousands of people missing in Assad's prisons, only to become prisoners themselves. Are the stories of the atrocities in the prisons exaggerated at all?"

"No", she responded. "My brother was missing for almost a month. We began to believe he died like so many other people. But luckily he showed up in the central prison in Hama city. For the past month they had been moving him from prison to prison.

Also, I know a man who used to protest with us. He was wanted and so he hid for a long time. Once he was visiting his parents and someone saw him. There are government 'rats' everywhere. Security forces came to the house and talked to his mother advising her to give him up. They promised her that they only wanted to ask a few questions. Unfortunately, she believed them and told him to come out and they surrounded him. She never saw him again.

There were also two brothers I know that also disappeared and I never heard of what became of them. A man from my neighborhood was arrested with his dad. His dad is old and had diabetes. They tortured both of them. The father died of thirst in his son's lap.

Another father of six kids was arrested at the beginning of the revolution. A few weeks later he was released. He was emaciated and spoke frequently about how terrible it is inside the prisons. He was arrested again shortly afterwards and we never saw him again. There are thousands of stories like these.

GUIDING QUESTION

Why is habeas corpus an important right?

PART FIVE

VOCAB

Kurds: "One of the indigenous people of the Mesopotamia plains and the highlands areas that today are contained within southeastern Turkey, northeastern Syria, northern Iraq, northwestern Iran and southwestern Armenia....After WWI and the defeat of the Ottoman Empire, the victorious Western allies made a provision in the 1920 Treaty of Sevres for the formation of a Kurdish state, to be known as Kurdistan. But their hopes were dashed three years later when the Treaty of Lausanne, which set the boundaries of modern Turkey, made no provision for a Turkish state and left Kurds with minority status in four countries—Turkey, Syria, Iraq, and Iran" (voanews.com).

GUIDING QUESTION

Why is oil important in the United States and how might this affect our decisions in the Middle East?

"What else could the UN do to help with this conflict or are their hands tied?", I asked.

"For my husband and I, we believe that the UN is just a lie.

Everyone knows how terrible it is in Syria and yet they still pretend that they need to investigate. For example, today I was reading that the UN sent aid to Syria but because of the political restrictions they sent it through an NGO that belongs to Assad's wife. In only five months they gave them millions. Now how did that benefit the Syrian people? They say there is no other way but that's just lies because they know this money will not help the people. It will help the government to still stand."

"That sounds very suspicious," I responded. "Do you think that America did enough, not enough, or too much in your country?"

"Honestly, we think America didn't do anything to help the Syrian people. Or actually they just made it worse. They tried to get involved with the Kurds to help them make their own country the way the Jews were able to establish their own country of Israel. But it did not work out for the Kurds. Unfortunately, because America supported the Kurds in their fight for their own country it only divided Syria more. This made the Kurds turn on the Arabs. Kurds raised the flag of Israel as a way to do whatever makes America more satisfied and to get more support. This turned the rebels fighting Assad against the Kurds. Instead of fighting the regime together they became enemies; and then America abandoned the Kurds. So the Kurds joined the regime again to stand against any other countries or factions or rebels or ISIS, even though Assad discriminates against the Kurds."

"I was surprised to hear that the Kurds supported the Assad regime," I responded. "I read that they had been forced to 'live without the rights to travel abroad, own property, or take university slots because the regime had long denied them national identification cards' (Lemmon 34). Why would they fight alongside a regime that discriminated against them in such a way?"

So you see the Kurds and the US, in the end, just helped to make sure the Syrian people would lose the civil war against Assad; that's it. I don't know precisely why. But I think that it is just a territory issue between Turkey, America, and everyone else. Everyone wants to control the oil in the northern parts of Syria. So the Kurds became essentially bodyguards for the oil for America in exchange for American support of them.

GUIDING QUESTION

Why is oil important in the United States and, according to Layla, how did this affect our decisions in Syria?

PART SIX

GUIDING QUESTION

When should citizens peacefully protest and when should they give up?

"Layla, what was the moment when you realized that you needed to leave Syria?" I asked.

"When protests stopped or became very rare, and it became more and more challenging to organize one, I decided to leave. There came a time when we lost hope and started to see how other countries getting involved was not about us anymore. Even if we protested, it didn't matter anymore, we felt that it was pointless.

In many cities, people were dying. You could see it on the news. The world was just broadcasting the news where it happened, the statistics of the casualties. Nothing was being done about it actually so many Syrians, including myself, gave up more and more.

I read that 2015 was the year that the highest number of people fled Syria. Bombings were everywhere. Government attacks were happening and the lies just continued. Countries said it was unacceptable but did nothing to help us.

For example, bombings were supposed to be a red line under Obama, but nothing happened. Obama did nothing about the bombings. Torture and death in prisons were supposed to be a red line for Obama but he did nothing. Back in 2011, President Obama released a statement that 'for the sake of the Syrian people, the time has come for President Assad to step aside' (Lemmon 34). But he never actually did anything about it. Gas attacks were supposed to be a final red line for

Trump; but Trump only responded to the sarin attack Assad dropped on the people of Ghouta with minor bombings of a military facility in Syria. These are some of the reasons why people lost hope, eventually, and I decided to flee."

"I see", I responded. "Assad never let up on the protesters. He kept arresting people, and torturing them, even using sarin gas against them, and there was no support for you from the international community. I can see why you decided to take your family and move to Turkey."

GUIDING QUESTION

Why did Layla decide that it was time to give up protesting and move to Turkey?

PART SEVEN

VOCAB
Salamiyah: A city in western Syria.

GUIDING QUESTION
Why might the kindness of strangers lift our spirits
when we are going through challenging times?

"Layla, how is your life in Turkey different from life in Syria?"

"In so many ways. Firstly, I have a very bad social life here for many reasons. I'm not fitting in with Syrians or Turkish people here in Turkey. But here, at least, I can dream of having a decent job. I can hope for my kids to have a better life. In Syria, if you want to succeed you need to either travel to work in another country and send money to your family in Syria, or become corrupt in some way. So here you have other options at least."

"What is the hardest thing about having to move to a new country?" I asked.

"I would say leaving the people I love behind. Knowing that some of them might die and I'll never see them again. Also, learning to adjust to a new country is difficult; the Turkish language is challenging. Another major challenge is trying to create a social network from zero. It is very hard."

"I am sure that there is a bright side. What is the best thing about being in your new home country, Turkey?"

"Compared to Syria, here in Turkey, I can dream to work, to do something important. I could be hired to work for someone who will appreciate me. For example, someone might hire me for the skills I acquired from my studies, the languages I speak, or the experiences I have. Also, Turkey is very beautiful, especially when compared to my home city which was small and limited. So here it is amazing!"

"Layla, would you ever return to Syria?"

"I honestly don't know. Sometimes I say never; sometimes I say maybe just to visit. I will not return anytime soon. For my sons' sakes I don't think I will ever move back there! But maybe ten or more years from now, maybe my family and I will visit; but maybe not."

"What final message do you have for American students?"

"You are the generation of the future. Hopefully, you'll do better than the people of today. So please, if you see a refugee, or any type of different person, try to be nice to them. Believe me, you might save a life or a future. Because sometimes I lose hope entirely. But then a small gesture, or some stranger, or a neighbor, or anyone, changes my day and my thoughts. We are people like you. We have dreams and hopes; we just need a chance in life.

You can make a difference so please try to."

GUIDING QUESTION

How can being kind to the people we encounter on a daily basis make for a better world?

A NOTE TO TEACHERS

After finishing the discussion questions in this reading, I recommend that you reach out to NaTakallam for a cultural interaction with a refugee from Syria. Offer students the opportunity to act as journalists by creating unique and culturally sensitive questions to ask during the interview.

This is the link to NaTakallam: https://natakallam.com/education/

PRINTABLE WORKSHEET FOR TEACHERS

Guiding Question	Answer before reading the section	Answer after reading the section*
Part 1: Why is freedom of the press important?		
Part 2: Why is freedom of speech and the right to peacefully protest important?		
Part 3: Why would an evil dictator want to portray himself as good to the international community?		
Part 4: Why is habeas corpus an important right?		
Part 5: Why is oil important in the United States and how might this affect our decisions in the Middle East?		
Part 6: When should citizens peacefully protest and when should they give up?		
Part 7: Why might the kindness of strangers lift our spirits when we are going through challenging times?		

---

* Guiding questions at the end of each section are sometimes reworded. Use a direct quote from the text to support your thinking.

CHAPTER FIVE

AN INTERVIEW WITH SALAM
FROM YEMEN

"In ancient times Yemen was known as Arabia Felix, Latin for 'happy' or ''fortunate'. It acquired the name because its high mountains attracted rain, making it more fertile than most of the Arabian Peninsula" (The Guardian). Why, then, are there more people dying of starvation and a lack of medical supplies than anywhere else in the world today?

According to UNICEF, Yemen is the world's largest humanitarian crisis. 21 million people in Yemen rely on assistance just to eat, including 11 million children (unicef.org). Much of this is due to the fact that Yemen has been at war since 2014. But why did the situation in Yemen get to this point? How did the war start; and why has it become such a major catastrophe?

The former president of Yemen is Ali Abdullah Saleh. He ruled Yemen for decades, starting in 1990, and publicly compared it to "dancing on the heads of snakes" (Reuters). During the Arab Spring in 2011, the Yemeni people protested, hoping for a better economy and less corruption in the Yemeni government. President Saleh was accused of corruption and of amassing between "32bn and $60bn during 33 years in power" (Al Jazeera). At the time. Yemen was among the poorest nations in the world. His brutal crackdown on protesters caused hundreds of deaths. "The protesters began to call upon President Ali Abdullah Saleh to resign" (Oxford Constitutional Law). He stepped down in February of 2012 due to pressures from the Gulf Cooperation Council (GCC). The GCC is a group of Arabic and Islamic countries that work together for political and economic purposes that benefit all members.

Saudi Arabia is the most influential member of the Gulf Cooperation Council (GCC). The other members are Bahrain, Kuwait, Oman, Qatar and the United Arab Emirates. This group of countries worked together to install a new government in Yemen, propping up then Vice President Abd-Rabbu Mansour Hadi as the new president of Yemen in February of 2012.

Even though the president changed, little else changed for the actual people of Yemen. The Houthis, a Shia Muslim minority group from northern Yemen who had participated in the protests against the rule of President Saleh, decided to fight back against the poor treatment they were receiving from the new government as well.

Even though the Houthis fought against ousted President Saleh, the old enemies, President Saleh and the Houthi rebels, joined forces against the new president, Hadi. Remember, the new President Hadi is backed by the entire GCC. The Houthis, supported by Iran, together with former President Saleh's allies, took over Sanaa, the capital of Yemen, in 2014. This sparked the ongoing civil war in Yemen.

President Hadi fled Yemen to Saudi Arabia for support from the GCC. Saudi Arabia and the UAE formed a coalition to return President Hadi to power.

Saudi Arabia had three war goals.

1. Restore Hadi as President.
2. Protect its southern border with Yemen.
3. Contain the growing influence of Iran in Yemen.

As a side note, Iran and Saudi Arabia are old enemies. Iran is a Shia country. Saudi Arabia is Sunni. These are two different branches of Islam with different rituals and beliefs about who should have been the first caliph (religious leader) when the Prophet Muhammad died. There have been many acts of violence between these groups since the death of the Prophet Muahammad in 632 A.D.

As of 2021, "the Saudi led coalition has conducted more than 20,100 airstrikes on Yemen since the war began, an average of 12 attacks a day. The coalition has bombed hospitals, schools, buses, markets, mosques, farms, bridges, factories, and detention centers" (hrw.org). "Since 2015, 18,000 Yemeni civilians have been killed or wounded" (apnews.com).

In 2015, the Saudi led coalition created a land, sea and air barrier around Yemen, preventing aid for the people of Yemen from entering the country. The Houthis are also blamed for blocking, taking and destroying aid meant for the people of Yemen. This is causing starvation, lack of medical supplies, and the spread of disease.

In 2017, after three years of fighting together against the Saudi coalition, the alliance of the Houthis and Saleh broke down. Saleh defected to the Saudi coalition live on television. Two days later he was assassinated by the Houthi rebels.

The Houthi rebels are openly supported by Iran; however, Iran denies supplying them with weapons or missiles of any kind. This is because the Houthis have been designated as a terrorist group and UN members cannot legally support terrorist organizations. Saudi Arabia, and others, insist that Iran must be smuggling weapons to the Houthi rebels since they are well supplied and missiles uncovered from a "Houthi strike in Saudi Arabia were proven to be Iranian made" (CNBC).

This is why Yemen is defined as a proxy war. Two rivals, Saudi Arabia (a Sunni Muslim nation) and Iran (a Shia Muslim nation) are backing opposite sides of another country's civil war. The US, France, and the UK have been supplying Saudi Arabia and the UAE with weapons and logistical support, while Iran supports the Houthi rebels. (Remember, both Iran and the Houthi rebels are Shia Muslims).

Many American senators urged both President Trump, and later, President Biden, to stop selling missiles to Saudi Arabia because of the humanitarian disaster it was supporting. Even though missile sales to the Saudi-UAE alliance were an injection for the American economy, the senators decried the fact that the missiles were being used against innocent civilians in Yemen. In February of 2020, Biden declared "'we're ending all American support for offensive operations in the war in Yemen, including relevant arms sales.' However, he said the US would continue to provide defensive support for Saudi Arabia against missile and drone attacks from Iranian-backed forces", meaning the Houthi rebels (The Guardian). In other words, Biden declared that the US will help Saudi Arabia if they are attacked; but the US will no longer sell them arms to use to attack Yemen.

Unfortunately, the situation in Yemen is continuing to unravel. In October of 2021, "the Houthis seized new territory in the oil rich provinces of Shabwa and Marib" (Al Jazeera). Fighting escalated in the summer and fall of 2021. In September of 2021, 10,000 people were displaced from their homes in Marib. The province of Marib is the internationally recognized government's last northern stronghold. If they lose Marib to the Houthis, they may likely lose the whole war. Violence, death, starvation and disease caused by the civil war continue to plague the people of Yemen.

PART ONE

VOCAB

Refugee: "A person who has been forced to leave their country in order to escape war, persecution or natural disaster" (Oxford Languages).

GUIDING QUESTION

How does war alter the lives of civilians?

SALAM'S STORY

Salam is a sweet and approachable young woman from Yemen. She is 28 years old. She has long dark hair that she ties back in a bun and large black eyeglasses that she often adjusts while talking. She has light skin that accompanies a kind smile and demeanor. She does not cover her hair.

Salam is a refugee of the Yemeni Civil War. In 2010, at 17 years of age, she left Yemen to study at a university in Turkey. The violence in Yemen started a few days after she left. Salam chose never to return home due to the violence, destruction and danger in Yemen that still continues. From 2015-2017 she lived in the United States for almost three years. She spent two years in California and one year in New York City. Today, she lives in Montreal, Canada.

I interviewed Salam on November 15, 2021.

We met via zoom. She was in Canada. I was in the United States. I started by asking her "what do you miss about Yemen and how has Yemen changed since the war started?"

"There are a lot of things that I miss about Yemen" she replied. "I miss the food. The food in Yemen is really good! I miss the quiet. I miss the weather. The weather there is very nice. It's not very cold like it is here in Montreal, Canada. There are six months of winter here in Canada. That's crazy! I prefer the weather in Yemen.

I grew up in Ibb, a town in the south of Yemen. It doesn't get too hot or too cold there. The weather is perfect."

"What is the typical forecast for Ibb?"

"Well, it's usually between 70° and 80°. It is sunny and warm; but it also rains sometimes. Mostly it's sunny; but it's a cool sun, not an extremely hot sun."

"Is there winter in Yemen? " I asked.

"In Yemen, it doesn't get extremely cold. It gets down to about 33° at the lowest."

"Does it ever snow there?"

"No no, it never snows."

"Can you tell me a little bit about the food?

"The food in Yemen has a lot of variety. There are a lot of different dishes. I miss the fact that most of the food in Yemen is homemade. Even when you go out to a restaurant most of the food that you get at the restaurant is made the same way you would make it at home. Some fast food is introduced to the culture, but it is not common."

"What did you do for fun when you were growing up in Ibb?" I asked.

"Ibb is a small town in a country where there isn't much to do. But we felt safe. In fact, we felt safe enough to send children to the supermarket. It's not like that in Yemen anymore."

"Can you tell me more about how life has changed in Yemen since the war began?"

"Well, firstly, things were much cheaper before the war. For example, when I was in Yemen it only cost 20 rials to take the bus from my home to school, which was a ten minute ride. Now they charge almost 100 rials for the same bus ride.

Also, people in Yemen were more relaxed before the war. Now people are very strict, especially when it comes to women and how they dress when they leave their homes because people are genuinely afraid that women may be harassed about how they are dressed. This is because there is no safety in Yemen. Everyone is very afraid; everywhere they go they feel afraid.

"I see", I responded. "A lot has changed in Yemen because of the war.

GUIDING QUESTION

How has the war in Yemen altered the daily lives of the people of Yemen?

PART TWO

VOCAB

Abaya: A modest, usually black robe, that goes over a woman's clothes. It has long sleeves and reaches her ankles.

Veil: Cloth covering a woman's hair and sometimes her neck.

GUIDING QUESTION

Why are women's rights important? What could go wrong if a woman could stand to lose her financial stability if she wanted a divorce?

"Salam, what are some of the pressures on women in Yemen now that there is an ongoing civil war?

"In Yemen, it's not just about religion, it's also about tradition. In Yemen, when women leave the home they are required to cover themselves. They have to wear an abaya and a veil. It's a bit different from city to city. In most cities in Yemen, women are required to cover their entire faces and only expose their eyes. When I lived in Yemen, 99% of women from my hometown in Yemen covered their entire faces when they left home. Since the civil war, the radical people have become more powerful in Yemen. It is a slippery slope because if it was up to the Houthi rebels women would not be able to leave their homes at all."

"Salam, what might happen to a woman who did not wear her hijab correctly, or what are some other reasons why women would be harassed over their attire in Yemen?" I asked.

"People in Yemen would think that if a woman was show-ing her face that she was acting seductively. The people in the street would make this very uncomfortable for her. Everyone would stare at her with disdain and yell at her. This is why most women just choose to do the easy thing and just cover their faces when they leave their houses.

"Could women be arrested for their attire in Yemen?"

"Yes, definitely they can. We have heard of some women getting arrested and sued for the way they dress. However, there is a bit of a paradox happening in Yemen now. Now that the Houthis have taken over there are certain additional restrictions on life, but we are also noticing that more women are going out in public with only the hijab covering their hair and necks, and not their faces. I would estimate that now about 80% of women cover their faces in Yemen and 20% choose not to. I think this is happening because people in Yemen are starting to have access to the Internet. They are starting to use Instagram and other forms of social media. This is especially true for the younger generation. They are starting to follow social media trends regarding how to look beautiful.

Also, the older generation of women in Yemen had to seek jobs to provide for their families during the civil war. The war caused inflation which made it extremely challenging for families to live on just one income. Many women created small businesses such as making pastries and birthday cakes. As women became more independent and went out to find work, they started to have more freedom, and this created a situation where women felt they could expose their faces in public."

"I see, now that more women have their own income they are starting to feel more confident showing their faces. How did you feel as a woman in Yemen?"

"I decided to leave Yemen because of how I was being treated as a woman. I didn't think I had a very good future ahead of me as a woman there. I always wanted to have more freedom. I also wanted to see the world. In Yemen, we watched a lot of TV. We spent a lot of time at home. TV exposes you to the world. You realize that there is so much going on. I wanted to live my life without men telling me what I should do with my body, how I should dress, or when I can go out. I wanted to try something else. I didn't see myself living that type of life in Yemen.

So I left Yemen when I was 17. I finished high school earlier than my peers. I was awarded a scholarship to go to a university in Turkey."

"Are you saying that women in Yemen are very controlled by their fathers and their husbands?" I asked.

"They are independent. Women do work in Yemen. They also go to school. But at the same time the authority of the father, brother, uncle and the husband controls what women are allowed to do."

"Could women get divorced if they wanted to in Yemen?" I asked.

"Yes and no. A woman could get divorced; but her husband would have to go to court with her. If he doesn't show up and a woman wants to get divorced without approval from her husband she has to request Khula. This is a unilateral ending of the marriage where women have to return the dowry and give up their right to any future financial support from the husband. She would have to give away everything she received from her husband when she was married. This could equate to an entire life's savings. It is a huge chunk of money she received when she was married. Usually, the bride takes the large sum of money and buys gold with it. She would then wear elaborate lavish gold everywhere she went. All of that jewelry would have to be returned if she was sued for Khula. Also, she has to explain to the court a valid reason why she needs to get divorced in order for the judge to allow it.

On the other hand, if the husband wants a divorce she would keep her money and jewelry from her dowry."

"Would she have to give away her property and her children?"

"Not her children, not the property. But according to Sharia Law, after the divorce the woman would get no additional financial support from the ex-husband."

GUIDING QUESTION

Why might the financial burden of getting divorced without the husband's permission pressure women in Yemen to stay in abusive and unhappy marriages?

PART THREE

VOCAB

Sanaa: Capital of Yemen

Emiratis: People from the United Arab Emirates

GUIDING QUESTION

Why is access to healthcare important?

"Salam, how did the war affect the people in Yemen?"

"Firstly, people can no longer travel easily. The main airport in Sanaa was bombed; unfortunately, it is still closed today because of this. Thus, people have to travel all the way to the south of Yemen, to Aden, to get to an airport. For many people, this is a very challenging commute. For my family, before the war the airport was only four hours away in Sanaa. Now it's about a ten hour drive to get to an airport from where my family lives in Yemen.

Also, the checkpoints set up throughout the journey really slow the trip down; and they can be quite scary. The truth is that you never know which group the checkpoint is set up by- it could be the Houthis, the international government, Al Qaeda or the Emiratis. These checkpoints are set up throughout the roads in Yemen and slow down the travel process tremendously.

When you finally get to the airport, there is only one airline that is running. Only the national airline of Yemen is working. Also, a lot of countries have stopped giving visas to Yemeni people; so it is very challenging to travel outside of the country at all. These countries are afraid that we are not temporary visitors, but that we will try to become permanent residents because we will not want to travel back home to a war zone. I know a lot of people who have needed to travel outside the country to hospitals to be treated. Unfortunately, they could not get the proper treatment because the travel to the hospital is so long, costly or impossible."

"That's terrible.", I responded. "What kind of medical conditions did people have in Yemen that were unable to be treated?"

"Well, honestly, it was mostly people who were injured in the war. My sister was injured twice in the war. She was unable to leave the country to receive treatment. If she left the country, she would have no medical insurance. Besides, as I mentioned, many countries closed their doors to Yemeni residents in need of assistance."

"I'm so sorry about your sister." I responded. What were the injuries that she suffered that she was unable to receive treatment for?"

"The first time she was injured was in 2015. She and her family were bombed at the hospital where they were visiting her mother-in-law. They were heading for the exit when a missile from the Houthi rebels hit the hospital. Most of her family's injuries were severe burns to the lower parts of their bodies. My niece lost two of her toes; she was treated with some basic care in Yemen. However, she is unable to get plastic surgery. She has to live with the fact that she lost two toes. As a young girl this really affects her mentally.

One year later, in 2016, my sister and her family were at home in Ibb. In the middle of the night, a missile destroyed the apartment complex they were living in. This missile was not a Houthi missile, this missile was from the Saudi Alliance. The missile completely destroyed the two apartment homes that were above my sister's apartment. The people living above her died in the attack. The entire building collapsed and my sister and her family members were trapped. After a few hours, they did manage to escape from the rubble with mostly broken bones; but my sister still endures serious nerve damage which is very painful for her. The government denied her request to leave the country to have her nerve damage treated. The Yemeni government claimed that her injuries did not qualify for assistance from the government. But the hardest part is that the whole family was mentally traumatized!

After that, they had to live with family members who were willing to take them in. It was a long two years before my sister managed to rent a new apartment. There is no homeowners' insurance or renters' insurance in Yemen; my sister will never fully recover from the financial burden of losing her home and all of her family's belongings. However, the people of Yemen come through to help each other in times of crisis."

"That is shocking!" I responded. "What was the intended target or the missile that hit your sister's home?"

"The target was a Houthi camp that stored weapons. But it wasn't even close to my sister's house. It was about a 15 minute drive away."

"That is a huge miscalculation by the Saudi alliance!"

"I know", she responded. "But they always do that. You hear stories about bombings in schools, hospitals and buses where they missed the target all the time. Yemeni people always do their best to move on. They are living with the leftovers of their injuries.

Another example of trying to move on is one of my nephews; he has hemophilia. His blood does not clot properly when he cuts himself. He needs weekly injections just simply to live as a kid and play. Before the war it was much easier for him to get these injections. Unfortunately, after the war, the injections are no longer available for him. This is because they became too rare and expensive in Yemen.

I am lucky that my family has survived and we have found a way to move on; but I know a lot of people have endured a lot of heart-aching tragedies in Yemen."

GUIDING QUESTION

How has the inadequate healthcare available in Yemen affected Salam's family?

PART FOUR

VOCAB

Solar Panels: A panel designed to absorb the sun's rays as a source of energy for generating electricity and heating.

WhatsApp: A free app for instant messaging that is often used by people traveling internationally.

GUIDING QUESTION

What types of things do you worry about regularly? Should you ever feel guilt about things you can't change?

"How did the war affect you personally?" I asked.

"Luckily for me, I did not experience the war first hand. I actually left Yemen shortly before the war started. I was in Turkey at a university. But my family experienced it first-hand. I was away; but I was always on the phone talking to them. It affected me deeply and it gave me severe anxiety. I was worried all the time.

I decided to go to therapy to treat my PTSD. I was in therapy for a year. The therapy sessions helped me immensely. It helped me to realize that I don't need to feel guilty that I'm living a good life in Canada with access to basic things such as electricity. I also used to feel helpless because I couldn't help my family. I used to feel that the money I sent to my family in Yemen wasn't enough. I used to feel like nothing would ever be enough unless I was able to remove my family from Yemen. Now I remind myself that it is out of my control, the war is not my fault, and that I deserve to have a good life.

Now I'm not worried as much as I used to be. But before, when the war started, I was always waking up every morning expecting to hear bad news. I was expecting to hear that someone died or was injured. I started each day expecting bad news.

My family and friends in Yemen contact me through *WhatsApp*. So every time I hear the ding of WhatsApp that notifies me that I have a new message on my phone, my heart sinks. I think Oh my God, what now? I just don't want to hear anything bad anymore.

But I think we just try to stay strong and get through it. All the Yemeni people that I know here in Canada, we all have this shared sense of guilt that we are living here in Canada and we have a nice life with everything available such as electricity and water. Whereas, in my hometown of Yemen, there is no electricity without solar panels, and for many years, there was no electricity at all."

GUIDING QUESTION

What gave Salam a lot of anxiety? How did she learn to let it go?

PART FIVE

GUIDING QUESTION

How is electricity important for our daily lives?

"Can you tell me a bit more about the lack of electricity in Yemen?" I asked.

"For most people in Yemen, for the past four years, there has been no electricity at all. Some Yemeni people are using solar panels that they purchased themselves and they are expensive. Not a lot of people can afford to buy them."

"That is absolutely terrible that the people have gone four years with minimal electricity. Here in the United States we get so frustrated when we lose power for a few hours or a few days because of a storm. We can't even imagine what it would feel like to lose power for four years."

"It is very challenging!", Salam responded. "When I was still living in Yemen, before the war, we had electricity. Often enough, it would cut out for an hour or two; but then it would come back. We were accustomed to being able to use things like refrigerators, microwaves, irons and blow dryers. But now, in Yemen, if people don't have a solar panel that supports the use of a refrigerator, then people don't even have a refrigerator. Some people use solar panels for only basic light; cheaper solar panels do not support appliances.

Also, I know this is a very small thing, but it is frustrating. When my sisters have to get dressed up to go to a wedding, they don't even have the electricity for a blow dryer for their hair. If they want to use a blow dryer they have to go to a hair salon.

This can be very frustrating for them because weddings are one of the few times when women in Yemen get dressed up and do their hair nicely because they do not have to wear hijabs to wedding celebrations. This is because weddings are not mixed; there are only women at the wedding receptions. Women have their own parties; men also have their own parties after the ceremony. The weddings in Yemen are so lavish. People really dress up. They wear the best dresses they have, and they do their hair very nicely, and they wear a lot of makeup. At weddings, that is where women show off the most.

Wedding ceremonies usually take place at the bride's home. The male family members of the groom's family and the male family members of the bride's family gather together at the bride's house. The fathers of the bride and groom fill out the marriage contract. After that, they set a date for the celebration. Sometimes they celebrate on the same day; other times they celebrate on a different day. A wedding in Yemen is celebrated for seven days. One night the celebration is at a large hall with a buffet, and the rest of the week the celebrations are at homes. The bride wears something different each day. It is a week long of festivities. It is important for women to have electricity to do their hair and otherwise prepare for the week-long wedding reception."

"What other types of struggles happen because of lack of electricity in Yemen?"

"There are also other necessities that are lacking. For example, my mother needs insulin for her diabetes. The solar panels that she had for a long time were not sufficient enough to operate the refrigerator. She had to store her insulin at a pharmacy. It was very inconvenient to have to go to the pharmacy each time she needed to take her insulin. Now, luckily, she has a solar panel that is high quality enough to run the refrigerator. The shortage of electricity is very frustrating and very costly."

GUIDING QUESTION

How does the shortage of electricity affect the lives of the people of Yemen?

PART SIX

VOCAB

Sanction: "An action that is taken or an order that is given to force a country to obey international laws by limiting or stopping trade with that country, by not allowing economic aid for that country, etc" (Merriam-Webster.com).

Import: Taking goods into a country.

Humanitarian Aid: The delivery of food and water, temporary shelter, and/ or health services to people in need.

GUIDING QUESTION

Why do countries impose sanctions on other countries and who do they really hurt most?

"Do you think it was right for Donald Trump to put the Houthi rebels on the terrorist list, causing Yemen to suffer from more sanctions?", I asked.

"This is a very difficult question to answer. If you ask this question to a group of Yemeni people they will be divided into two groups. Personally, I do not think it was what was best for the people of Yemen. This is because once the Houthi rebels were on the terrorist list, it caused many sanctions to be placed on the country. Sanctions make life very hard for the people of Yemen. They cause a lot of humanitarian aid to be unable to get to the people of Yemen. Unfortunately, in Yemen, we do not produce most of the products that we consume. We import them. So, if there are sanctions, it becomes very hard for us to get goods.

Further, the economy in Yemen is so bad that many people are not being paid at all. Many people are working just to keep their jobs, in hopes that eventually they will be paid again at some point. They are hoping that one day the Houthi rebels will go away and their lives will go back to normal.

Another major concern is medicine. People died because of the sanctions and the lack of medical supplies getting into Yemen. It is really difficult now to get the medicine that you require in Yemen. This is because on top of the sanctions, the Houthi rebels are not allowing aid to come into the country. They want to control what comes in and what goes out. It's not just the sanctions; it's also the blockade on the country.

On the other hand, having sanctions on the Houthi rebels will make it more difficult for them to be successful. It will be more difficult for them to import weapons. But they will find a way.

Some people agree with putting them on the terrorist list because it will be more challenging for them to stay in power and they think it will cause them to eventually give up. Or they might be more willing to negotiate an end to the war. But in the meantime, the people who are not involved in politics, the people who just want to live their lives, are affected by the sanctions."

GUIDING QUESTION

What is the long-term goal of the sanctions on Yemen and who do the sanctions really hurt?

PART SEVEN

GUIDING QUESTION

How does it make you feel when your parents or government control what you do?

"Salam, as a follow-up to that, who do you side with in the Yemeni Civil War?"

"I don't side with anyone. I just want the war to end. There shouldn't be a war in the first place. I see it as both sides are wrong. Well, I suppose, a small side of me sides with the recognized government of Yemen because at least it would keep the international Republic of Yemen in place."

"If the Houthi rebels win, do you think life would be worse for women, or the people of Yemen in general?" I asked.

"It will be worse for everyone! The Houthis are very controlling" Salam replied. One small example of the ultimate control of the Houthi rebels is that women cannot take birth control pills without their husband's permission."

"What if the woman is not married?"

"Well", she laughs, "in my culture women are not supposed to be on birth control if they are not married. Another example is the separation of the genders at universities. The community in Yemen is very conservative. However, in universities the classes are co-ed. But ever since the Houthis took over, my niece told me that there is one side of the classroom designated for women and another side for men.

When she went to class, my niece just took the first available seat. But she realized that she was sitting closer to the boys than the other girls were. After a while, she noticed that the girls were giving her dirty looks and acting as if she was trying to be seductive by sitting near them. This wasn't happening before the Houthi takeover."

"Salam, what if a male and female met at a university, could they date each other without the permission of their families?"

"Well, people in Yemen do date each other. They just can't date each other in public. There is a lot of secret dating that goes on in Yemen. For example, groups of girls and groups of boys meet up at coffee shops. A male and female who like each other arrange to be in the same place at the same time with their friends. The couple would never be alone; but it would essentially be an open secret that the boy and the girl were there to meet up with each other.

If a young man is interested in marrying a young woman the man's family is supposed to ask the father of the woman for her hand in marriage. The parents of the bride have the final say regarding whether a marriage will take place. If the father doesn't make the decision, then the brother or the uncle will make the decision.

GUIDING QUESTION

How are the people from Salam's hometown controlled by the Houthi rebels and how are they controlled by their families? What emotions do they probably have about this? Why?

PART EIGHT

VOCAB

Offensive missiles: Missiles fired at an enemy.

Defensive missiles: "A system, weapon, or technology involved in the detection, tracking, interception, and destruction of attacking missiles" (Wikipedia).

International pressure: When countries take measures to coerce another nation into behaving a certain way or taking a certain action.

GUIDING QUESTION

What should come first in the US, morals or money?

"Do you think the termination of missile sales to Saudi Arabia from the US will have an effect on the war and the people of Yemen?"

"From the conversations I have had with my close friends in Yemen, it is not going to have much of an effect on the war at all. Most of the missiles that Saudi Arabia buys from the United States are defensive missiles. In other words, they are not offensive missiles that are used to attack the people in Yemen. But, hopefully, it will put international pressure on Saudi Arabia to terminate the war. On the other hand, if they don't buy weapons from the US they will just buy them from another country."

"That is interesting. I didn't realize most of the missiles we sold to them are defensive missiles. I thought I had heard that the missile Saudi Arabia used on the school bus in Yemen was American made?"

"Yes, that is true. On Aug. 9, 2018, the Saudi coalition used an American-made bomb, accidentally hitting a school bus, and killing 40 children. But most of the missiles purchased from the US are defensive missiles that are used to shoot incoming missiles out of the sky."

"What was the reaction on the ground of the people of Yemen regarding the school bus?"

"Everyone was heartbroken and in shock! I can't speak for everyone, but I remember that my family members were keeping the kids from going to school for a while out of fear that something could happen to their buses or their schools. It made us feel as though nobody really cares about us Yemenis and our civil war. I mean really, who blows up a school bus!! Why would anyone in any war do that!!! It's just madness."

GUIDING QUESTION

Selling weapons to Saudi Arabia was an injection for the American economy; but was it moral and ethical?

PART NINE

VOCAB

Iran Nuclear Deal: Aka- Joint Comprehensive Plan of Action (JCPOA) "On July 14, 2015 the P5+1 (China, France, Germany, Russia, the United Kingdom, and the United States), the European Union (EU), and Iran reached a Joint Comprehensive Plan of Action (JCPOA) to ensure that Iran's nuclear program will be exclusively peaceful" (https://2009-2017.state.gov.jcpoa).

The agreement, made under the Obama administration, removed sanctions placed on Iran since 1979 in exchange for a promise that Iran's nuclear program would only enrich up to 3% uranium, enough for electricity, not a nuclear weapon. This agreement was made, in part, because in 2012 Iranian President Ahmadinejad threatened to "eliminate" Israel, an ally of the US (https://www.jcpa.org/jl/vp536.htm).

GUIDING QUESTION

How can the ballot citizens cast for president in the US affect the citizens of other nations?

"How has the change of the American president from Trump to Biden affected the situation in Yemen?" I asked.

"Well, the current administration and the previous one had two different policies. Trump put the Houthi rebels on the terrorist list which caused sanctions. Biden took them off the list, but little has changed for the actual citizens of Yemen.

What may happen is that Biden could possibly attempt to end the war by including the war in Yemen as part of the nuclear deal with Iran. Many of my friends forecast that Joe

Biden might suggest that Iran can take over Yemen if Iran promises never to have a nuclear weapon. For the Yemeni people this would not be good because this would mean that the Houthi rebels would take over Yemen. But it's politics, it's messy, no one knows for sure what may happen next."

"Wow that is an interesting theory!" I responded. "Do you really think that Biden might just give up on Yemen so that he can get back into the nuclear deal with Iran?"

"I don't know if it's giving up on Yemen; but it might be what Biden thinks is best for the world."

"What if the Houthi rebels win the Civil War in Yemen on their own, without Biden's help, do you think Iran might still have a lot of influence over Yemen in that scenario?"

"Of course! They already do; and I think it's wrong. I am angry that Iran and Saudi Arabia are fighting each other in my land. They are not destroying their home countries, and their citizens aren't dying. They are destroying my country and the citizens of my country are suffering. I don't want the Houthi rebels to win and ultimately for Yemen to be controlled by the Houthi rebels and Iran. I am angry about what they have done to my country and I don't want them to control my family."

"Salam, do you think this is wrong because you think the Shia in Iran might change the religious ideology in Yemen?"

"The ideology is already changing. We never used to talk about who is Sunni and who is Shia before the Houthi rebels started the civil war. I inherited the religion of Islam; but I don't consider myself to be Sunni or Shia. When the Shia Houthi rebels took over we started to see the different rituals that the Shia participate in and we were a bit confused because we had never done those types of rituals. So the religious dynamic in Yemen is changing already; but that is not my main concern. My main concern is freedom and integrity for the people of Yemen."

GUIDING QUESTION

How can the ballot we cast for president here in the US, affect the citizens of other countries?

PART TEN

VOCAB

Proxy War: "A proxy war occurs when a major power instigates or plays a major role in supporting and directing a party to a conflict but does only a small portion of the actual fighting itself" (brookings.edu).

GUIDING QUESTION

Do government officials always make choices that benefit mankind; or do they sometimes put their personal goals first?

"Salam, what are your thoughts about the fact that the governments of Saudi Arabia and the United Arab Emirates give money to help with the famine in Yemen but also are responsible for the bombing and causing much of the devastation in Yemen?"

"That's a good question. Well firstly, they are hypocrites. Secondly, they are not fighting Yemen. The civil war in Yemen is a proxy war. As I mentioned, Saudi Arabia and the UAE are fighting against Iran over Yemen. Saudi Arabia and the UAE are only helping to aid the starving Yemeni people because they want to have control over the Yemeni people. It's hypocrisy.

I hear that there is a lot of aid entering Yemen from Saudi Arabia and the UAE, but who does it really reach? I also think it is about control. They help fund us so they can help make our decisions for us. Saudi Arabia and the UAE focus on controlling the south of Yemen. They have interests there. The Saudis and the Emiratis see no benefit in the south of Yemen being a stable and economically thriving part of the world. If southern Yemen is not involved in a conflict it would have time to flourish and trade. Saudi Arabia and the UAE want to have the most authority and control in the Middle East. If Yemen thrives economically, it could challenge Saudi Arabia and the UAE for control in the region."

GUIDING QUESTION

If Salam is correct about the intentions of Saudi Arabia and the UAE, is this ever how leaders of a nation should behave? Why or why not?

PART ELEVEN

VOCAB

International Community: "The countries of the world considered collectively" (Oxford Languages).

Diplomatic Relations: "A relationship between two countries in which they send diplomats to work in each other's country" (macmillandictionary.com).

Marib: An oil-rich city which is the last government stronghold in the north of Yemen. The Houthis have taken the capital, Sanaa, and all of the other territory in the north of Yemen.

Political Parties: "A group of people with similar political goals and opinions. The purpose is to get candidates elected to public office" (yourdictionary.com).

People's Congress: The ruling political party of Yemen since 1993.

Islah Party: A political party in Yemen that joined forces with the internationally recognized government of Yemen to fight against the Houthis.

GUIDING QUESTION

Why is it important for a country to be united?

"What would the real consequences be if the Houthi rebels manage to take the entire city of Marib?"

"The internationally recognized government of

Yemen is controlling the south of Yemen. However, most of the cities in the north are controlled by the Houthi rebels. It is only the city of Marib that is not controlled by the Houthi rebels in the north. So if the Houthi rebels manage to take the city of Marib they will essentially have taken over the entire north of the country. This will mean that they have won the civil war in Yemen and the international community will have to engage in diplomatic relations with the Houthi rebels."

"So, Salam what you're saying is if they take Marib, they win?" I asked.

"Not exactly, it will mean the country is divided and if they take Marib they would control the entire north. There would still be another fight; but the south of Yemen would most likely become a different country. The Houthis would take over the north of the country and the internationally recognized government would control the south.

There is also the Islah Party to contend with. The Islah Party is fighting the Houthi rebels as well. The Houthis are trying to get into Marib. But the internationally recognized government of Yemen has created a blockade surrounding all of Marib to keep the Houthis out. The Islah Party also does not want the Houthi rebels to take over the entire city of Marib and the Islah Party may try to take over their own part of the city."

"I have a clarifying question for you," I responded. "Is the Islah Party aligned with the internationally recognized government?"

"No, not officially, but they help fight the Houthis. They were allies of the Yemeni government; but then they had a falling out. The falling out was a disagreement about policy. Before the war in Yemen, the Islah Party was the opposing party to the internationally recognized government of Yemen. The previous president Ali Abdullah Saleh of Yemen was from the People's

Congress party and the Islah Party was the opposing party. But later, in 2016, after President Saleh's assassination by the Houthis, they worked together."

"What was the reaction of the people of Yemen to Saleh's assassination by the Houthis?", I asked.

"My gosh! I still remember that day. It was really divided. Some people were really happy because he betrayed the Houthis live on television. Other people were really, really, really sad and depressed. Many people were shocked! My mother was really sad! It was one of the few times when I heard my mother's voice over the phone sounding that sad. She was upset that he was killed in such a brutal way. He wasn't just shot, he was also thrown on the back of a pickup truck. My mother was a supporter of him. Remember, she lived during the good old days, when Yemen enjoyed peace. She believed that he brought a lot of good things to the country. The younger generation does not agree, for the most part.

When I checked social media, some people were happy and some people were really sad that he was assassinated by the Houthis. One of my friends was a journalist who worked for a newspaper that was opposing Saleh and his party. His newspaper was always criticizing the government and President Saleh's policies; but even he was really depressed when Saleh was killed."

"It's interesting that the internationally recognized government is also divided. That makes sense regarding how the Houthi rebels were able to take over Sanaa and start a civil war, a country divided is easier to fight and destroy," I said.

"It is normal for a country to have two political parties," Salam responded. "For example, in the United States, you have the Republicans and the Democrats. But imagine there was a Civil War in the United States and the Democrats and the Republicans had to align themselves with each other, against an enemy, just to keep the integrity of the government. That is what is happening. The People's Congress and the Islah Party had to join forces against the Houthi rebels."

"I need to ask another follow up question" I stated. "As you know, the US has halted its support for offensive missions out of Saudi Arabia and the UAE and into Yemen. Do you think that the United States should continue to support the defense of the Saudi/ UAE coalition against the Houthi rebels?"

"In some ways, yes. For example, internationally the Houthis are still recognized as rebels and rebels/terrorists should not be allowed to attack others. On the other hand, I don't think they should. This is because the war needs to stop! They should just decide to end the war, regardless of anything else."

Five days after I interviewed Salam the Houthis claimed they fired 14 drone attacks at several Saudi cities. Saudi Arabia's news agency reported 13 return attacks into Yemen.

GUIDING QUESTION

Why is it important for a country to be united?

"Salam, what is one message you have for American students?"

"Don't believe the media. Don't believe the news. If you want to know something about a country, it doesn't have to be Yemen, any country, just go and look at the right sources. Don't just use google. Review other sources such as books and credible newspapers. Read the story from different perspectives, not just one perspective, so you could have a full picture of what happened."

PRINTABLE WORKSHEET FOR TEACHERS

Guiding Question	Answer before reading section.	Answer after reading each section[*]
Part 1: How does war alter the lives of civilians?		
Part 2: Why are women's rights important? What could go wrong if a woman could stand to lose her financial stability if she wanted a divorce?		
Part 3: Why is access to healthcare important?		
Part 4: What types of things do you worry about on a regular basis? Should you ever feel guilt about things you can't change?		
Part 5: How is electricity important for our daily lives?		
Part 6: Why do countries impose sanctions on other countries and who do they really hurt most?		

---

[*]   The question may be worded differently at the end of the section. Use a direct quote from the text to support your thinking.

Guiding Question	Answer before reading section.	Answer after reading each section*
Part 7: How does it make you feel when your parents or government control what you do?		
Part 8: What should come first in the US, morals or money?		
Part 9: How can the ballot citizens cast for president in the US affect the citizens of other nations?		
Part 10: Do government officials always make choices that benefit mankind; or do they sometimes put their personal goals first?		
Part 11: Why is it important for a country to be united?		

As a possible culminating activity, visit the NaTakallam website to request an hour-long zoom experience with a refugee from Yemen—you may be assigned Salam herself! Make sure to inform NaTakallam that you read this chapter from *Refugee Realities.*

This is the link: https://natakallam.com/education/

Above: Biden's visit to Israel: 2022
Below: Children's Monument at Yad Vashem: The pillars are not fully grown because the children never reached adulthood before they were murdered during the Holocaust. The pillars are positioned as students typically are positioned when taking a class photo at school.

CHAPTER SIX

ORIT AND SALMAN
FROM ISRAEL AND FROM THE WEST BANK (PALESTINE)

The nation of Israel is considered to be Holy Land. However, this small piece of contested land, the size of New Jersey, has caused a tremendous amount of death and devastation. Many fear it will be the cause of World War III.

Today, Israel is a Jewish nation that was established for Jews following the Holocaust- the murder of 6 million Jews during WWII. Many people view Israel as a necessary refuge. These individuals believe that if the Jews have their own Jewish nation, where they can protect each other, there will never be a Holocaust again.

Israel boasts a world renowned Holocaust museum, Yad Vashem. The name Yad Vashem refers to the Old Testament and this name was chosen to honor the lost victims of the Holocaust with a "memorial and a name". The employees and tour guides at Yad Vashem work tirelessly to honor those who perished by telling, and retelling, the names and stories of the victims of the Holocaust. They often speak openly about their own family members that they lost during the Holocaust, usually while fighting back tears.

This is one of the cattle cars that was used to transport Jews to the death camps. It is positioned on the grounds at Yad Vashem. A Holocaust survivor could see it from her kitchen window when it was placed there and it made her immensely sad as it dredged up terrible memories. Yad Vashem assisted her with moving to a new home with a better view.

Israelis of all ages, and people from all over the world, visit this museum to honor the victims and the righteous individuals who helped Jewish people survive the Holocaust. Many visitors to Yad Vashem leave the museum with a renewed understanding of how propaganda can cause hate and lead to violence.

Jews from all over the world move to Israel to be with other Jewish people in the only Jewish nation that exists in the world today. This is referred to as making "aliyah" to Israel. The land of Israel was selected by the UN as a place for Jews fleeing Europe following World War II because many people believe that this land was promised to the Jews by God in the Old Testament of the Bible.

Most Palestinians disagree with using the Old Testament as evidence for Jewish rights to Israel because it is not unbiased, scientific evidence. Further, many Palestinians claim

Dome of the Rock—Built over the location of the original Temple in Jerusalem. King Hussein of Jordan sold one of his villas in London to pay the $6.5 million to coat the Dome in gold.

that after the Holocaust the Jews "bit the hand that fed them" because Palestinians helped the first Jewish refugees of WWII, and eventually they displaced many Palestinians. Additionally, many Palestinians argue that the Promised Land mentioned in the Old Testament is actually Yemen.

Jerusalem, the capital of Israel, is the holiest city for the Jews. They believe that Moses was a prophet who delivered the Jews out of bondage in Egypt during the 13th century BC. According to the Old Testament, he used his mighty staff to part the Red Sea for the Jews to cross through, escaping the Egyptian soldiers, fleeing to safety, and ultimately settling in Israel. Many Jews believe that the Ark of the Covenant held Moses' staff, the mana, or everlasting food the Jews ate while traveling out of bondage from Egypt to Israel, and the 10 Commandment Tablets. The Ark of the Covenant was placed in the Temple in Jerusalem until "586 B.C. when the Babylonian Empire conquered the Israelites, and the Ark, at the time, supposedly stored in the temple of Jerusalem, vanished from history" (National Geographic).

Dome of the Rock

Prior to 586 B.C., the Ark was housed in the Holy Holies which is the location of the Dome of the Rock at the Temple Mount today. This is the place Jews believe God is most present in the world. The Ark of the Covenant is important to Jews, Christians and Muslims alike; thus, they all revere this same location where the Ark of the Covenant was once housed. (pictured avove, the ark was housed under the golden Dome)

Eastern Jerusalem is also critically important to the religion of Islam for another reason. The Temple Mount compound, pictured above, also houses the Al Aqsa Mosque, the third holiest mosque in the world, for Muslims. It is built across from the Dome of the Rock.

The Dome of the Rock is also the location from which Muslims believe the Prophet Muhammad took his famous night journey to heaven, visiting the seven tiers of heaven and witnessing the beauty of God's throne. Muslims believe the Prophet Muhammad did this from the foundation stone,

Al Aqsa Mosque

over which the golden Dome of the Rock was later built. They believe he did this without dying, and it is an important miracle for Islam. He left earth from the same creation stone that Jews believe is "the place where creation began, and the site where Abraham was poised to sacrifice Isaac" (smithsonian-mag.com). The Old Testament story relates that Abraham was poised to sacrifice his son Isaac, the son he had with his wife Sarah, per God's request, and as a test of his devotion to God. At the last minute, the Angel Gabriel came to Abraham to stop him. A ram appeared for Abraham to sacrifice instead of Isaac.

Muslims tell this story differently. Muslims believe Abraham almost sacrificed Ishmael, not Isaac. Ishmael was his son with his concubine, Hagar. Muslims believe Ishmael to be the father of the Muslims. Jews believe Isaac to be their direct relative. Also, Muslims believe this famous test of Abraham's faith, when he was asked to sacrifice his son, actually happened in Mecca, Saudi Arabia. Mecca is the holiest Muslim city, as

opposed to the Jewish belief that it happened at the creation stone in Jerusalem.

Today, Jordan controls the Temple Mount, where the foundation stone is located, in Eastern Jerusalem.

The West Wall is Judaism's holiest place of prayer. The Dome of that Rock is behind it. (Pictured above)

The West Wall is part of the Temple Mount's retaining wall, built by Herod the Great in the first century B.C. It is as close as the Jews can get to the Holy Holies (Dome of the Rock) for prayer, other than going underneath the wall.

Notice the walkway at the top right of the photo on page

161. It is the non-Muslim entrance to the Temple Mount where the Dome of the Rock is actually located. Only Muslims can pray on the Temple Mount. Non-Muslims are not allowed entry into the Al Aqsa Mosque or the Dome of the Rock. However, non-Muslim tourists can enter the Temple Mount compound and take photos of the outside of these buildings.

When the Jewish nation was created in 1948, many Palestinians (mostly Muslims) were displaced. The Palestinian people refer to this as the Nakba, or catastrophe, because they suddenly lost their homes and many of them became destitute. Many Palestinians still believe that they have the right to

return to the homeland of their ancestors. Also, in the 1967 Six-Day War, Israel annexed territories from Jordan, Syria and Egypt. The territories they still occupy are the West Bank, which they took from Jordan, and the Gaza Strip, which they took from Egypt. These territories are predominately Palestinian territories and have been under Israeli occupation ever since. Palestinians living in these territories live under Israeli control but do not have the right to vote for representatives in the Israeli government. Groups such as Hamas in the Gaza Strip, and Hezbollah in the West Bank, often use violent measures to try to fight for the right to return to their homelands, and other Palestinian causes.

There is an ongoing conflict in Israel between the Palestinians and the Israelis over territory. The Israelis built a wall separating them from the Palestinian territories in the West

Bank and Gaza in an effort to prevent terrorism. They began building the wall in 2002 due to an uptick in violence towards Israeli settlers including suicide bombings, bus bombings and knife attacks. On the next page are pictures of the wall from the Palestinian side in the West Bank.

(Notice the Israeli lookout towers pictured on the next page.)

The Israelis have been accused of arbitrarily arresting Palestinians, denying them access to parks and beaches, and shooting protesters and journalists. Israel has stated that Iran supports the Palestinians with missiles and other supplies. Iran denies this. The US supports Israel with billions of dollars in funding and military equipment each year. "Under the current deal, the US has agreed to give Israel about $3.8 billion in military assistance annually" (USA Today).

This graffiti on the border wall in the West Bank is of the Palestinian-American journalist Shireen Abu Akleh who was shot dead by an Israeli soldier while on assignment in the West Bank.

Why is there a conflict in Israel?

Review the timeline below for historical clarification of how the conflict began and morphed over the years.

A RECOMMENDATION FOR TEACHERS

When reviewing the timeline, have students write Jews, Christians, Muslims, or ancestors of Muslims after each date to help them have a visual of who controlled Israel and when.

C. 1800 B.C.

The Hebrew Tribes first arrive. (Jews)

597 B.C.

The Babylonians (Today Iraq) conquered the Kingdom of Judea and destroyed the First Temple, built by Solomon. The Ark of the Covenant was lost forever. Many Jews left the area.

70 A.D.

The second Jewish Temple, built by Herod the Great, was destroyed by the Romans. The West Wall, where Jews pray today, is all that remains of the Jewish Temple.

691

Muslim armies defeated the Byzantines to conquer Jerusalem. The Dome of the Rock was built on the ruins of the Jewish temple that is believed to have held the Ark. Jews, Christians and Muslims all believe the story of the Ark of the Covenant. Jews and Christians were allowed to visit as pilgrims until the 10th century.

1099, Crusaders Capture Jerusalem

The first crusade, launched in 1095, sought to conquer the Holy Land for Christendom. After the capture of Jerusalem in

1099 many Jewish, Christian, and Muslim residents were massacred. The Muslim General Saladin retook Jerusalem in 1187; Christian rule in the Holy Land ended with the fall of Acre to Muslims in 1291.

1516

Ottoman Turkish rule began and lasted for almost 400 years.

1918, Balfour Declaration

The British captured Palestine from the Ottomans and declared its support for a Jewish nation there.

1948, Declaration of the State of Israel

Following the 1947 decision of the UN's General Assembly to petition Palestine into two states, one Arab, and the other Jewish, violence in engulfed the country. Ben-Gurion's provisional Jewish government declared independence, and British forces withdrew. About 700,000 Palestinian Arabs, fled or were forced from their homes."

1967, Six-Day War

The Israelis received word that they would be attacked by Syria, Egypt and Jordan. They launched a preemptive strike and captured the Golan Heights from Syria, the Sinai and the Gaza Strip from Egypt, and the West Bank and East Jerusalem from Jordan.

1994, Oslo Peace Process

The process gave the Palestinian Authority control of the West Bank and Gaza towns. (The Sinai was returned to Egypt in 1982.) Israel continues to occupy the West Bank and Gaza, and ultimately controls these regions. Tensions continue to flare and conflicts arise regularly. (Eyewitness Travel)

There has been a recent escalation in violence in Israel and Gaza in May of 2021. This is because a Palestinian neighborhood known as Sheik Jarrah, located in East Jerusalem, has become extremely controversial. In 1980, "Israel passed the 'Jerusalem law', stating that 'Jerusalem, complete and united, is the capital of Israel', thereby formalizing its annexation of East Jerusalem" (Tahlan 2). Since the annexation, there have been disputes over the rightful owners of several neighborhoods in Jerusalem. It has gone on for decades.

In 1982, a lawyer for Palestinian residents of Sheik Jarrah signed an agreement stating that the Sheik Jarrah neighborhood did indeed belong to two Jewish trusts. However, the Palestinian residents would be allowed to remain living there as protected tenants who were to pay rent to the Jewish trusts that owned the land. Shortly thereafter, the Palestinians stated that their lawyer was tricked into signing the agreement and thus they stopped paying the rent as a form of protest. The two trusts that owned Sheik Jarrah sold it to the Nahalat Shimon Settler Association who decided to evict the Palestinians from the territory for not paying their rent. Between 2002 and 2017 over 40 Palestinians were evicted from Sheik Jarrah. On May 7, 2021 there were clashes at the Temple Mount over a forthcoming court case that was likely to evict 13 more families, a total of 58 people, 17 of whom were children. If evicted, these families would likely become homeless. The court decision has subsequently been delayed and was the spark that ignited the 11 Day Conflict that consumed May of 2021 in Israel.

During the 11 days of violence, "253 Palestinians were killed, 66 were children. 13 Israelis were killed, including one child" (Humaid).

I spoke in depth to a female Israeli soldier, Orit, and a Palestinian man from the West Bank, Salman. Their perspectives vary greatly, but they both long for the same thing, peace.

INTRODUCTION TO THE ISRAELI SOLDIER

O rit is a female Israeli soldier in her late 20's. She grew up on a large family farm in a small village located in the center of Israel. As a girl, she enjoyed going to school and playing soccer. Her father raised sheep and chickens. Most of her father's business partners were Arabs who frequently purchased sheep from her family farm. She regularly socialized with Arabs at her home. When her father celebrated his birthday he received presents from Arabs and when her family was in the mood for pizza they frequented Arab restaurants because they love the fresh Arab ingredients. She forged many solid relationships with Arab people over the years.

Orit enjoyed growing up in Jerusalem because it is the birthplace of her religion, Judaism. She cherishes living near the West Wall and physically standing in the same place where Abraham, the father of Judaism, once stood.

Growing up, she knew that she would be required to serve in the Israeli military in some fashion. She chose to enlist in the Israeli Navy where she held several positions. After serving in the navy she traveled around the world and then decided to journey to the United States for a job working for the Jewish Alliance of Greater Rhode Island for a stint of two years. I invited her to speak to my students in the state of Rhode Island several times. She always has a warm and inviting expression; her message reaches teenagers easily because her sincerity shines through via her demeanor and warm tone. When she talks about Israel she lights up as she is enamored with a true love for her country. She often told me that I should travel to Israel and see it for myself. Further, Orit invited me to come to her home for dinner when I do visit there and she highly recommended that I swing by her sister's candy shop for authentic Israeli candy.

Orit describes Israel as not a war zone, just a stressful place to live. She was eight years old in 2000, the year the Second Intifada happened. This was the second large conflict with Israel. The village she grew up in is actually very close to an Arab village. Sadly, there were a lot of terrorist attacks in her village. She remembers feeling very afraid then, even to walk down the street. She regularly saw soldiers stationed in her village for Israeli protection and she knew that there were regular attacks on buses and bus stations. This was scary for her to come to terms with as a child. Even being at home was a scary part of her childhood because every Israeli home that has been built since 1982 is required to have a shelter. This made her quickly realize that the walls of her home were not enough to protect her from possible bombardments. As an adult, she knows that a peaceful day in Israel can change quickly; but she tries not to worry too much about the security situation anymore.

As a young adult Orit became a commander in the Israeli Navy. In fact, she was one of the first female commanders of a patrol boat. Holding this position meant that she was on the front lines of navy conflicts. In 2014, when she was working on a missile ship she took part in an important operation on the Red Sea where she captured a large Iranian cargo ship. From outside of the ship it looked as if it was carrying construction supplies. However, inside the ship were six-foot missiles that were supposed to be shipped to Sudan, smuggled into the Sinai Peninsula of Egypt, and then into Gaza. This load of rockets was probably a very small percentage of the true amount of missiles that Iran was shipping to Gaza.

Also, on the beach in Gaza there was an intense shooting battle. An Israeli soldier was shot and killed. Orit heard the voice of the commander over the radio system. She could hear the fear in his voice and she was praying that it was not someone she knew that was killed. She labels this experience as a traumatizing event because it made her realize that the army is not a game. She said, "Sometimes, it feels like Sony PlayStation because you don't see your enemy and you don't realize what's happening because you can't look into their eyes. But when I heard the voice of the commander, and I could hear the fear in his voice over the radio, it made me understand how real the situation is. It gave me a deeper understanding of what I am doing and that I should be as careful as possible, and do everything as if I am doing surgery, to make sure that I inflict the least amount of harm possible."

Orit's sister is an officer in the Iron Dome. In fact, she met her husband, a fellow officer, while working there. The Iron Dome is a system of the Israeli army in cooperation with the United States Army and it is the only major system that defends the civilians in Israel. It creates a safe dome so that missiles that come into the area are responded to with an anti-missile to destroy it and keep the civilians safe. Currently, Israel sells the Iron Dome to countries around the world.

The officers in the Iron Dome try to calculate where the missile is heading and where it can be crushed so that there is a safe area that it will land in. The officers do their best to assure that the missile does not land in a city, or a suburb, or an area where there are people. It is a very advanced system; but mistakes can occur.

It is unusual to hear warning sirens near Tel Aviv or Jerusalem; but people who live close to Gaza hear them almost every day. Sometimes their sleep is interrupted over and over all night. They have to wake up and run down to the shelters in their homes often.

Today, Orit continues to work for the Jewish Alliance of Greater Rhode Island, the smallest state in the United States. In early May of 2021, Orit returned to Israel to celebrate her sister's wedding, only to quickly discover that Israel was unraveling. The controversy over the Sheik Jarrah neighborhood, and the siege at the Al Aqsa Mosque, quickly spiraled into an 11 Day Conflict in her home country. Her sister's wedding was able to proceed, although there was a siren wailing prior to the ceremony. The bride, an Iron Dome officer, screamed "JUST RUN" and she and all of her bridesmaids had to run outside and lay on the ground covering their heads because the wedding venue did not have a bomb shelter. Luckily, the bride's wedding dress wasn't ruined, just a bit wrinkled. After being terrified, they decided to return for the wedding service and laugh it off as a story for the bride's grandchildren.

Orit's flight back to the United States was delayed because of the bombing of Israel's main airport, Ben Gurion, by Hamas. She returned to the United States on May 22, 2021, I was able to meet with her shortly thereafter.

INTRODUCTION TO SALMAN

Salman is 30 years old and he does not consider himself to have grown up in Israel; he refers to the West Bank as Palestine. He believes that the city he grew up in, Nablus, is in Palestinian territory.

Salman went to school and played soccer and board games such as Chess with his friends. His classmates and he also played a unique version of the game "Cops and Robbers." They called it "Palestinians and Israelis". The goal of the game was to capture each other.

His life was very different from the lives of Israeli citizens. There was no easy back-and-forth for him between Israel and the West Bank. He could not regularly travel to the Al Aqsa Mosque in Jerusalem to pray because he was not allowed to through the border wall into the Israeli region. He was also never able to travel to the Dead Sea, a tourist attraction visited

Dead Sea

by Americans almost every day. Further, he has never seen the Mediterranean Sea on the west coast of Israel because of the long process of asking Israeli permission to travel there.

He described his life as normal but plagued by frequent bad news. His school was often closed because of the conflict with Israel, especially in 2000 when the Second Intifada happened. One of the students at his school was killed along with one of his teachers. Another one of the teachers at his school was arrested by Israeli soldiers. The teacher was taken to an Israeli prison for being a member of Hamas, a group Israel labels as a terrorist organization. Salman labels Hamas as the resistance for resisting the Israeli occupation of Palestinian land. According to Salman, Palestinians were arrested frequently where he grew up. It was something that he became used to; but he did not agree with it. Salman believes that Israelis have no right to arrest Palestinian residents and place them in Israeli prisons.

Palestinians see Hamas more as a protest movement; whereas, Israelis tend to compare it to Al-Qaeda or ISIS. Salman firmly disagrees with the terrorist label and instead considers Hamas as part of the Palestinian community. Young Palestinians who join Hamas often think they have to resist the Israeli occupation. Salman explains "they don't want to fight but they want to resist for their rights, not to take rights from others, but for their own rights."

Salman had trouble finding work in the West Bank because of the poor economy. He traveled to Saudi Arabia for work, and then back to the West Bank through the Jordanian border several times. He does not enjoy traveling through the border with Jordan. He complains that he frequently gets stuck there, unable to pass for hours or even days.

He also worked in the UAE and Turkey before finally settling in Argentina. He dislikes the cold in Argentina and longs for his family and friends in Nablus, West Bank. Salman misses the large family gatherings his family often held and his more than 30 cousins. He misses living near them and the close relationships with his large family are challenging to keep up with while living half a world away. He also longs for his close friends that he met while studying at the university in Nablus.

Currently, Salman teaches Arabic online to students all over the world. He is also working on his master's degree, specifically a master of Complex Systems through UTT, which is a French university.

His first opportunity to speak to an Israeli person actually happened after he moved to Argentina. The only Israelis he ever saw in the West Bank were soldiers and what he referred to as armed settlers who had moved there. He never spoke to them and they never spoke to him while he lived in the West Bank.

Salman encouraged me to visit the West Bank. He told me that when I travel there he will send his brothers from Nablus to meet me in Bethlehem and show me around. He explained that his brothers could bring me to the Church of the Nativity, which is the church built over the location of Jesus' birth. He also explained that his brothers will bring me to the best restaurants with the most delicious food in Nablus, and that the prices of everything are very cheap in the West Bank, especially compared to the more expensive Israeli city prices. He explained that I should not fear terrorism in the West Bank. Americans travel there safely all the time and many Americans were working at the University in Nablus that he attended. He admitted that it is a conservative city; but Americans are welcome.

When Salman speaks about the Palestinian and Israeli conflict you can hear the passion in his voice. His enthusiasm for expressing the Palestinian perspective is pervasive. When he spoke to my students they were enamored by the authentic, robust and enlightening conversation we held.

VOCAB

Arab: "The Arab World consists of 22 countries in the Middle East and North Africa: Algeria, Bahrain, the Comoros Islands, Djibouti, Egypt, Iraq, Jordan, Kuwait, Libya, Mauritania, Lebanon, Morocco, Oman, Palestine, Saudi Arabia, Qatar, Somalia, Sudan, Syria, Tunisia, the United Arab Emirates and Yemen" (middleeastpdx.org).

Israeli: "A native or inhabitant of the Republic of Israel" (webster.com). This usually refers to a Jewish person living in Israel.

Palestinian: "Belonging or relating to the region between the River Jordan and the Mediterranean Sea which used to be called Palestine" (collinsdictionary.com). People who live in the West Bank and Gaza today are referred to as Palestinians.

This usually refers to a Muslim person living in the West Bank or Gaza.

Intifada: The Palestinian uprising against the Israeli occupation of the West Bank and Gaza Strip. The First Intifada was in 1987. The Second Intifada was in 2000 and lasted until 2005.

Hamas: A group located in the Gaza Strip. It "is designated as a terrorist group by Israel, the United States, the European Union, the United Kingdom, as well as other powers" (BBC News). Palestinians refer to Hamas as the resistance against the Jewish occupation of Israel.

I interviewed Salman on May 26, 2021.
I interviewed Orit on May 28, 2021.
Below are the questions that I asked Orit and Salman. I asked them the exact same questions to get a deeper understanding of how their perspectives vary based on their upbringings and religions.

GUIDING QUESTION

After reading each question, and the responses from Orit and Salman, reflect deeply about how their answers are similar, and how they are different. Ask yourself which response resonates with you more, or if they resonate with you equally, and why.

A NOTE TO TEACHERS

Teachers may wish to have their students fill in the graphic organizer after reading the responses to each question. They could also participate in a think, pair, share activity after each question.

	How are the responses similar?	How are the responses different?	Which response resonates with you more, or do they resonate with you equally? Why?
Question 1: What are your thoughts about the border wall between Israel and the Palestinian territories? Is it necessary and effective?			
Question 2: Why did the protests at Al Aqsa mosque turn violent on May 7, 2021?			
Question 3: Can you tell me more about the neighborhood of Sheikh Jarrah? How long have the families lived there and where will they go if they are removed? What is the situation there now?			
Question 4: Did Hamas make a fair request when it asked the Israelis to withdraw from the Al Aqsa Mosque compound by 6:00 on May 10, 2021 or there would be violence?			
Question 5: Was the date of the scheduled Jerusalem Day Parade coinciding with the end of the month of Ramadan a main cause of the 11 Day Conflict?			

	How are the responses similar?	How are the responses different?	Which response resonates with you more, or do they resonate with you equally? Why?
Question 6: What was the reaction on the ground where you were when Hamas fired its first rockets towards Israel?			
Question 7: Can you talk about the reaction on the ground where you were when Israel fired its first rockets towards Gaza?			
Question 8: Why do you think Hamas has 50,000 missiles at this time?			
Question 9: How long do you think Hamas has had rockets?			
Question 10: Why do you think that Hamas was firing rockets into Israel but Fatah, Hezbollah and the Palestinian Authority stayed out of it?			
Question 11: Do you think the situation would've changed if the US intervened militarily during the 11 Day Conflict? What could the US do or have done?			

	How are the responses similar?	How are the responses different?	Which response resonates with you more, or do they resonate with you equally? Why?
Question 12: During the 11 Day Conflict we heard about a lot of violence in several homes and neighborhoods between Arabs and Israelis. What could have been done to prevent this?			
Question 13: Some American media news outlets claim that Israeli soldiers should not respond with violence when they are attacked with rocks and Molotov cocktails. Do you agree?			
Question 14: During the 11 Day Conflict, Netanyahu stated that he could only continue bombing or invade Gaza. Why did he make this statement?			
Question 15: Do you think it was necessary, and is it really true, that Israel bombarded entire neighborhoods in Gaza?			

	How are the responses similar?	How are the responses different?	Which response resonates with you more, or do they resonate with you equally? Why?
Question 16: Do you think the conflict has ended with the cease-fire and what do you think will happen next?			
Question 17: Do you think the cease-fire could have happened sooner?			
Question 18: Both Hamas and Israel are claiming victory in the 11 Day Conflict. Who do you see as the victor?			
Question 19: What do you believe should become of Israel, the West Bank, and Gaza in the future?			
Question 20: Is there a chance that the conflicts over Israel could escalate into a third world war?			
Question 21: What is one message you have for American students?			

QUESTION ONE

What are your thoughts about the border wall between Israel and the Palestinian territories? Is it necessary and effective?

RESPONSE FROM ISRAELI SOLDIER

"First of all, there are different levels to the border. There are actual border walls and there is also fencing. We monitor the borders to make sure that there are no terrorists that cross into Israel. Part of the border is an electronic fence with cameras above it to monitor who comes close to the border and who might plan to cross it. It's just there to make sure that terrorists don't cross the border.

We also have a border with Egypt in the south and with Jordan in the west. We have borders with them even though we have peace agreements with them. We also have a border with Syria and Lebanon.

Unfortunately, Hamas built tunnels under the border wall from Gaza into Israel. They built these tunnels underground so they could cross the border without being spotted. In 2014, they crossed the border through the tunnels and engaged in terrorist attacks against soldiers and civilians in the Jewish border towns. Thus, in 2017 the Israeli government decided to build an anti-tunnel border. They built a wall 6 to 10 meters underground. That stopped the tunnels because they couldn't build the tunnel and cross through the border wall that was built underground.

Honestly, I wish I could tell you that I don't believe in a border wall and that we don't need one. Unfortunately, these situations do happen and have happened. We never know when a terrorist attack will happen. We have had terrorist attacks on holidays and weekends when we didn't expect to be attacked. Unfortunately, we have to do what we have to do to keep our civilians safe. Try to imagine what it would feel like if there were underground tunnels from Canada coming into the United States and people crossed the border, without anyone knowing, to attack you and civilian people.

There are many Palestinians who travel from Gaza and the West Bank into Israel easily for hospitalization. For example, the leader of Hamas has recently been diagnosed with cancer and he has moved to Israel to receive medical treatment there. Just a few days ago he was shooting rockets towards Israel, and he killed many Israelis, and now he's coming to Israel for medical treatment."

RESPONSE FROM CITIZEN FROM THE WEST BANK

"The border wall was inspired by Prime Minister of Israel Ariel Sharon. He thought this would keep the Palestinians away from the Israelis. But, just a few months ago Human Rights Watch classified that wall as an apartheid system. This is the international name for the wall there. It is just like the wall that was in South Africa. But the real reason for the wall is to isolate the Israeli community. The Israelis don't want to hear anything about the Palestinians. They don't want to see or hear anything about what's happening to the Palestinians in their territories. The idea and the construction of the wall is 100% illegal. If a Palestinian destroys a part of that illegal wall, the Palestinian will be arrested by the Israelis. I feel very badly about the wall.

The border wall is probably effective for the Israelis; but it is illegal under international law. Palestinians cannot pass through the border for work, for hospitalization, or even to visit the beach. It is as if they are living in the world's largest prison. Instead of building a wall, Israel should make peace with us and make a nice, happy and healthy situation for both Israelis and Palestinians.

For example, I always wanted to travel to Jerusalem and see the Al Aqsa Mosque for myself. I tried several times but my request to pass through the border was denied. I was only able to make it through the border one time. This one opportunity happened because I traveled through the border with a group of university students; however, it was very difficult to travel there. There were several checkpoints between my home city and the border wall. There are unnecessary checkpoints throughout the West Bank. Even if you only desire to travel from your city to a city 5 km away you will come across a checkpoint.

If I actually wanted to travel from the West Bank to Gaza it would be impossible because of the number of checkpoints that would slow me down. Gaza has been completely locked down for 15 years. Many Gazans have died because they are not allowed to pass through the checkpoint to go to the hospital in Israel. The hospital in Gaza is not nearly as well equipped as the ones in Israel are. Thus, as a Palestinian, I certainly do not think that the border wall should remain."

QUESTION TWO

Why did the protests at Al Aqsa mosque turn violent on May 7, 2021?

VOCAB

Judea and Samaria: The terms used by the Israeli government to refer to the occupied West Bank.

TikTok: A popular video-sharing social network service.

Ramadan: The ninth month of the Muslim calendar. Muslims follow strict fasting and abstinence from sunrise to sunset. Eid al Fitr is the celebration held at the end of the month.

RESPONSE FROM ISRAELI SOLDIER

"The protest at the Al Aqsa Mosque was not just a protest. It was a violent protest. There were Arab and Palestinian people throwing rocks and stones at the Israeli police, and fighting with them with fireworks.

All the media said was that the Israeli soldiers stopped the protesters and it was never explained why the soldiers had to stop the protesters. Israeli soldiers are trained to only use violence when there is a specific reason for it. At the Al Aqsa Mosque the situation became violent. Protests are fine. Everyone can protest. It just depends on how you decide to protest. You cannot use violence to protest.

Also, there was a TikTok trend happening where Palestinian and Arab people walking through Jerusalem would slap, and commit other acts of violence, against Jewish people. It became a funny joke to post videos of this on TikTok. There were many followers of this trend. Any Jew who was in the traditional costume of the Orthodox Jew might be slapped, videoed and posted on TikTok. The Jews were often on the ground being assaulted and the Palestinians were laughing. It was a minor form of terrorism to walk in the street and slap someone just because they are Jewish.

Ramadan was also happening at this time. This is a month when Muslims fast during the day. They eat at night and they have celebrations as well. At this time, in the center of Jerusalem, the TikTok trend to assault Jews was becoming more and more common. The Israeli police tried to prevent these attacks by limiting Palestinian movement in certain areas. The Muslims became very angry because they felt that they were being denied their freedom of movement. Then Israel decided to open all the streets again.

Hamas rules in Gaza but they also have branches in Jerusalem, Samaria and Judea. You refer to Samaria and Judea as the West Bank. Hamas felt that they had to support the pro-tests at the Al Aqsa Mosque; thus, Hamas fired rockets towards Jerusalem. This is when the Israeli government said 'enough is enough. You cannot shoot rockets towards our capital city', and we retaliated against Gaza by firing rockets back at them."

RESPONSE FROM CITIZEN FROM THE WEST BANK

"First of all the protest at the Al-Aqsa Mosque happened during the month of Ramadan. During this month, the Mus-lims sleep more and work less. For Muslims, this is a very spir-itual month. It's not a month for making problems. During Ramadan, Palestinian Muslims really want to go and pray at the Al Aqsa Mosque. According to international law, they have the right to go and pray there. Unfortunately, some extrem-ist Israelis wanted to break into the Al Aqsa Mosque grounds during the month of Ramadan. This would be like breaking into the Vatican at Christmas. Why would non-Christians do such a thing at Christmas?

First, the Israelis closed the main road to the mosque. There were young Muslim men there who became angry that this road was closed. Don't forget, about 90,000 people were traveling to pray at the mosque, closing a major road would cause significant traffic. Of course, some of the young Muslim men became angry. So at least one of them threw a rock at the police. The police answered with grenades and guns and more violence.

They started to remove Muslims from the mosque. There are many videos of this. The soldiers went into the mosque with their shoes on. This is a serious sign of disrespect at a mosque. Then the soldiers threw grenades inside the third holiest mosque of Muslims. Even if they don't believe in Islam, they should be respectful of Muslims. It is a religion of 2 billion people. Why would they do such a thing when the people were already tense about the Sheik Jarrah neighborhood problem?"

QUESTION THREE

*Can you tell me more about the neighborhood of
Sheikh Jarrah? How long have the families lived there
and where will they go if they are removed? What is
the situation there now?*

VOCAB

Sheik Jarrah: A neighborhood in Eastern Jerusalem that is
being disputed by the Palestinians living there and the Jewish
owners of the land.

Nakba: The Palestinian word for "catastrophe". It refers to
"the events of 1948 when many Palestinians were displaced
from their homeland by the creation of the new state of Israel"
(Oxford Languages). The state of Israel was created for Jewish
refugees of World War II and to offer Jewish people a homeland.

North Korea: A nation in Asia that is known for human rights
violations. The people of North Korea do not have freedom of
speech, travel, employment, religion and usually endure forced
labor.

RESPONSE FROM ISRAELI SOLDIER

"Jewish people bought the Sheik Jarrah neighborhood
located in Eastern Jerusalem in 1968. Palestinians took money
for their property because they were displaced from Sheik
Jarrah. Later, Palestinians moved back into this neighborhood;
but they were not paying rent to the Jewish owners of the land.

Try to imagine if you had a property where people didn't
pay you rent for a long time. Obviously, the landowners decided
to evict them. The decision is now in the hands of the courts.
I really trust the courts in Israel and that they will make the
right decision regarding the property in this neighborhood.

Unfortunately, the Palestinians feel as if the Israelis are trying to unreasonably move them out of the Palestinian area of Jerusalem and make it for Jews; but this is not the case. The Palestinians failed to pay their rent and so they are being evicted."

RESPONSE FROM CITIZEN FROM THE WEST BANK

"The problem of the Sheik Jarrah neighborhood started in 1948 when the Nakba happened and Israel became a nation. Many families from places such as Haifa and Jaffa in northern Israel, became refugees without a home. They moved to Eastern Jerusalem and settled into neighborhoods, such as Sheik Jarrah, which were not yet part of Israel. These neighborhoods did not become part of Israel until 1967, following the Six-Day War.

Recently, Israeli courts decided to evict them. There has been an ongoing court dispute over the Sheik Jarrah neighborhood. The Israelis claim that the lawyer for the Palestinians living in Sheik Jarrah signed a document agreeing that the Palestinians were not the owners of the neighborhood and in fact they were renters of the property. The Palestinians are claiming that the lawyer signed this document without their knowledge.

The UN has called for Israel to stop the eviction of Palestinians from this neighborhood because it is a human rights violation that is prohibited under international law. Just because a document came from the court of Israel doesn't make it legal. Many European countries have asked Israel to stop these evictions. But Israel has its own agenda.

Think about this, do you believe in the court of North Korea? There is really only democracy for the Jewish people, not the Palestinian people in Israel. Israel touts itself as the only democratic nation in the region. This is a lie actually. There is no democracy if you classify people by their religion. If the international community does not get involved the Palestinians will lose their neighborhood."

QUESTION FOUR

Did Hamas make a fair request when it asked the Israelis to withdraw from the Al Aqsa Mosque compound by 6:00 on May 10, 2021 or there would be violence?

VOCAB

Jerusalem: The capital of Israel, it is the holiest city for Jews and Christians. It is the third holiest city for Muslims. (Explained in the introduction)

RESPONSE FROM ISRAELI SOLDIER

"No matter what, such a request is never fair. Hamas should have said 'let's sit and talk.' They should never fire rockets at anyone."

RESPONSE FROM CITIZEN FROM THE WEST BANK

"Hamas only gave Israel a few hours warning to withdraw from the Al Aqsa Mosque and that was very demanding. However, they had already warned the Israelis several times prior to that for the past few weeks to be more respectful of the Al Aqsa Mosque. Muslims began to worry that the Israeli community might destroy the Al-Aqsa Mosque. Hamas felt pressured by the entire world to respond and they decided to fire six rockets towards Jerusalem. All of these rockets were stopped by the Iron Dome. Hamas knew that these rockets would be stopped by the Iron Dome. They were just sending a message."

QUESTION FIVE

Was the date of the scheduled Jerusalem Day Parade coinciding with the end of the month of Ramadan a main cause of the 11 Day Conflict?

VOCAB

Jerusalem Day Parade: Jerusalem Day is celebrated on the 28th of Iyar, according to the Hebrew calendar, or in proximity to that date. On June 7, 1967 (the 28th of Iyar, 5727), in the course of the battles for Jerusalem in the Six-Day War, east Jerusalem was liberated from Jordanian rule and came under Israeli sovereignty.

One or two days before the holiday, a festive parade is held in Jerusalem, entitled "Rural Communities Salute Jerusalem. Thousands of people march in the parade, mostly members of kibbutzim and moshavim and rural education institutions" (main.knesset.gov).

RESPONSE FROM ISRAELI SOLDIER

"No, it was not the main cause. The 11 Day Conflict happened because there were a lot of different problems happening at once such as the TikTok trend to assault Israelis and the controversy over the Sheik Jarrah neighborhood."

RESPONSE FROM CITIZEN FROM THE WEST BANK

"This became one of the main causes for the conflict. The scheduled Jerusalem Day Parade coincided with the end of the month of Ramadan which is a very holy time for Muslims. They knew that this was a very important religious time for Muslims. They could've selected a different date. But they chose this date to provoke the Palestinians.

The parade was canceled after the conflict with Hamas started. I think this parade should be canceled forever. This parade is very racist. During the parade they celebrate taking Jerusalem from the Arabs. I think this parade should be canceled at least inside of Jerusalem because it provokes Palestinians and it is a very sensitive region and topic."

QUESTION SIX

What was the reaction on the ground where you were when Hamas fired its first rockets towards Israel?

VOCAB

Tel Aviv: A historical tourist hub and beachfront city on the Mediterranean coast of western Israel. It was the location of the American Embassy in Israel before the Trump Administration moved it to Jerusalem.

Gaza: A Palestinian section of Israel located in the southwest, along the border with Egypt. Hamas headquarters is located there. The civilians in Gaza live under an air, sea and land blockade and survive in dire economic conditions since Gaza was occupied by Israel in the 1967 Six-Day War.

IDF: Israeli Defense Force- army, air, and navy forces- their main focus is the protection of Israelis.

RESPONSE FROM ISRAELI SOLDIER

"First of all, in Israel, every day, there are rockets fired at southern cities from Gaza. When the six rockets were fired towards Jerusalem I was, honestly, preoccupied with my sister's wedding that was happening the next day. When I first heard about it I thought it was the typical rockets that are usually fired towards the villages in the southern part of Israel. I didn't realize that it was fired at our capital just yet.

The day of my sister's wedding was very scary. We were at a beautiful wedding venue northeast of Tel Aviv. My sister, Eve, was getting married. She is an officer in the Iron Dome. Her husband is also an officer in the Iron Dome. That is how they met. Before the ceremony Eve was getting ready with me and our three other sisters. The groom was in a different room preparing as well. Suddenly, we heard the air raid siren that warns Israelis that there is a rocket fired towards us. It is very rare to hear a siren northeast of Tel Aviv. It is much more common closer to the border with Gaza and in the south of Israel. It felt very surreal to hear the siren and at first we just looked at each other in fear. I asked Eve if she thought it was real and she just screamed 'Run out!! Just run out!!' So we opened the door and we ran out and we asked each other 'where are we going to run to? There's no shelter here.' Since we were in the center of Israel there was no shelter at the wedding venue because it is very expensive to build and it is very rare for the center of Israel to be attacked. My sister Eve advised that we should just lie down on the ground and in our fancy bridal attire, we all just laid down on the ground and covered our heads. My younger sister gets regular tutorials at school regarding what to do when they hear the sirens go off. She knew that she should cover her head and she told the rest of us to do so. My little sister started screaming and crying. We all decided to pray together and look towards the horizon. We heard sirens one after the other. This was informing us that there were multiple missiles, not just one. We watched the missiles coming out of the Iron Dome and hitting the missiles that were coming out of Gaza. The ground shook and we could feel the vibrations from each rocket that was crushed mid-air by the Iron Dome Missile Defense System. Luckily, no one was hurt. It was terrifying.

Amazingly, the bride was the calmest among us because she works in the Iron Dome so she is used to this kind of stress.

In my family, we try to make light of difficult situations. After the sirens stopped, and the coast was clear, we decided to look at the situation positively. We had an amazing story to tell our grandchildren in the future. We were able to celebrate the wedding and the entire ceremony happened, as planned. When we returned home that night we heard another siren around 3:00 A.M. Thank God, we have a shelter in our basement at home. We went down there where we were safe.

The next day we began listening to the TV all day long to find out about what was happening. There was an orange alert on the right of the screen that warned if there was a missile heading towards villages and cities.

This conflict really affected Eve's wedding because at least 60 of her friends who work at the Iron Dome were not able to attend because of the 11 Day Conflict. Some of her friends came at the beginning of the wedding but then they received phone calls that they needed to go to the reserve immediately. Other friends of hers were unable to come to the wedding at all because they were in Gaza.

Israelis were horrified when they discovered that Hamas has rockets that can fire such a long range. But we really trust the IDF that they will do their job to keep our civilians safe."

RESPONSE FROM CITIZEN FROM THE WEST BANK

"Let me use a metaphor to explain the Israelis and the Palestinians. When I was in high school growing up in the West Bank, I was a tiny and thin guy. My group of friends were also tiny and thin guys. There was a group of male students who were very large and muscular. They used to bully us all the time. For example, if I laughed at a joke they would hit me.

One day, one of my friends got very tired of the bullying. He went up to the biggest bully and slapped him in the face. Unfortunately, all of the large boys beat him up terribly. But to my group of friends, he was a hero. We were so proud that he dared to slap the bully in the face.

My friend who had dared to slap the bully is like Hamas. The world was impressed that Hamas stood up to Israel. People in Gaza are unarmed. They are unable to defend themselves. All they have are rocks. Even though Hamas knew that the rockets fired towards Jerusalem would be stopped by the Iron Dome, and would do no harm, it was symbolic, just like the slap on the face of the large bully. Palestinians were happy that Hamas stood up to the bully, Israel."

QUESTION SEVEN

Can you talk about the reaction on the ground where you were when Israel fired its first rockets towards Gaza?

RESPONSE FROM ISRAELI SOLDIER

"Personally, when I heard that Israel was firing rockets into Gaza, I thought to myself thank God that we have the IDF to keep our civilians safe. My reaction was a strong feeling of desire for this conflict to end. I longed to go back to peaceful times. For some Israelis who live near Gaza, at night they go to sleep and the siren wakes them up at least six to ten times per night. They have to alert themselves and run to the shelters in their houses. It is crazy.

I listened to Israelis who had varied opinions on the television networks during the 11 Day Conflict. Some Israelis said that we should stop bombing Gaza no matter what. Others called for Israel to use all the force that we have. This is a very difficult decision to make because you are actually talking about life and death here, for both Palestinians and Israelis.

When you actually live in Israel, and you hear the air raid sirens for yourself, it is absolutely terrifying. Depending on where you live in Israel you may have up to a minute and a half to run to a shelter if you hear the air raid siren. For example, one of the times I heard the siren during the 11 Day Conflict I had to attend to my grandmother who was walking very slowly towards the shelter. This was a very scary incident because I knew that we were taking more than a minute and a half to get to the shelter.

It is difficult to live in Israel because you never know when you might hear the air raid siren or where you might be.

Some Israelis were so terrified by the 11 Day Conflict that they were calling for a complete destruction of Hamas in order to have peace. Other Israelis argued that we could try to destroy Hamas but all of Hamas and its sympathizers could never truly be destroyed. We don't want to be at war, or be in a conflict, we just want to protect ourselves. We don't want to harm anyone; but we don't want to be harmed either. Unfortunately, the question of how best to attain peace remains to be answered."

RESPONSE FROM CITIZEN FROM THE WEST BANK

"I was angry because I knew the reasons for bombing Gaza were wrong. Israel claimed that it bombed Gaza to stop Hamas from firing rockets towards Israel. But this makes no sense because they were not able to successfully stop Hamas with bombardments and they have never been able to successfully stop Hamas. For example, in 2009 there was a very bad war against Hamas but they were not able to stop Hamas from firing rockets. They killed hundreds of people. In 2012 the same thing happened again and Hamas did not lose its capabilities. In 2014 the same thing happened and Hamas did not lose its capabilities. Clearly, they know that they can't stop Hamas by bombing it, so why do they keep trying to stop Hamas with bombardments?

When Israel started to bomb Hamas they only wanted to kill civilians to put more pressure on Hamas. They wanted the Gazans to blame Hamas for the death of their friends and relatives.

Israel has amazing intelligence capabilities. In fact, they were calling and texting many civilians in Gaza to let them know that their homes were about to be destroyed by missiles. I was very angry when I heard about all of this terrible treatment of the Gazans by Israel."

QUESTION EIGHT

Why do you think Hamas has 50,000 missiles at this time?

VOCAB

Iran: A Shia Muslim nation bordering Iraq. Iran sympathizes with the Palestinians and is constantly at odds with Israel. Fears of Iran obtaining a nuclear weapon that may be used against the US ally, Israel, culminated with the Iran nuclear deal signed by the Obama Administration but revoked by the Trump administration. The Biden Administration is working towards rejoining the deal.

RESPONSE FROM ISRAELI SOLDIER

"First of all, Hamas is a terrorist organization. It is not a country. This organization's vision is to destroy Israel. That's the reason why they have missiles and rockets and weapons. Why do they have so many- because they want to destroy Israel. If they didn't want to destroy Israel then they would be able to sit down and talk about what we could do together.

Iran puts a lot of funds towards supplying Hamas with missiles. I feel terribly sad for the people of Gaza. I am sure that it is very scary for the civilians who live in Gaza. Hamas intimidates the civilians in Gaza. If you don't agree with them, they will kill you. It doesn't matter if you're a Palestinian or a Christian, no matter what, if you don't agree with Hamas the solution is to kill you.

Israel actually pays millions of dollars a year to support Gaza for humanitarian reasons such as medical supplies and to rebuild buildings that were destroyed in attacks. We send these funds to Gaza but unfortunately, the money often falls in the hands of Hamas and they use this money to build rockets. This is not just a small terrorist organization; it is huge. They build rockets that can shoot as far as Tel Aviv. Iran gives them a lot of money-, smuggles rockets into Gaza, and trains them with the vision of destroying Israel."

RESPONSE FROM CITIZEN FROM THE WEST BANK

"No one knows how many missiles Hamas has. If Hamas says that they have 50,000 missiles that could very well be military propaganda. It's normal for militaries to exaggerate to try to appear strong. But no one knows the actual number of missiles they have. We have to take into account the fact that Hamas has been locked inside of Gaza for 15 years. They have no resources to make the missiles. They redesigned missiles that Israel launched into Gaza that didn't explode. This is one of the big resources for them."

QUESTION NINE

How long do you think Hamas has had rockets?

RESPONSE FROM ISRAELI SOLDIER

"They have had rockets for a very long time. Unfortunately, every few years they receive and create and purchase more and more rockets which are more and more advanced and have longer ranges. Every time we have a conflict Israel destroys most of the weapons that Hamas has; but then they rebuild again."

RESPONSE FROM CITIZEN FROM THE WEST BANK

"Hamas has had rockets since about 2003. The first rocket they had was homemade. It was more like fireworks. It was weak but it was one way to resist the Israeli occupation. Hamas decided that no one will help the Palestinian resistance and that they have to resist on their own. They realized that they had to rely on their own expertise.

Hamas decided to do whatever it could to resist the Israeli occupation. For example, Hamas knows that for every anti-missile that is shot from the Iron Dome it costs Israel anywhere from $50,000-$100,000. The Israelis and the Americans pay this money. It is a form of resistance to financially burden Israel."

QUESTION TEN

Why do you think that Hamas was firing rockets into Israel but Fatah, Hezbollah and the Palestinian Authority stayed out of it?

VOCAB

Oslo Accords: The Oslo Accords (1993-1995)-were signed under President William Clinton to offer the Palestinian Authority limited self-governance of parts of the West Bank and the Gaza Strip.

Fatah: A Palestinian Social Democratic Party founded in 1959. Its headquarters are in the West Bank.

Palestinian Authority (PA): A Muslim group that is controlled by Fatah. It is an interim self-government with partial control over the West Bank and Gaza as established in the 1993-1995 Oslo Accords.

Hezbollah: A Lebanese Shia Islamist political party that supports the Palestinians. Lebanon is Israel's neighbor to the north.

RESPONSE FROM ISRAELI SOLDIER

"To correct you, it was not just Hamas. In Gaza there is also a second terrorist organization known as The Jihad which also shot rockets into Israel. I would also argue Hezbollah shot some rockets into the north of Israel during this 11 Day Conflict.

Fatah and the Palestinian Authority stayed out of it because they rule in the West Bank. The relationship between Israel and the West Bank is better than Israel and Gaza. I assume that they stayed out of the conflict to try to keep the relationship as it is."

RESPONSE FROM CITIZEN FROM THE WEST BANK

"First of all, Hezbollah is in a very complicated situation. If Hamas asked them to get involved in the situation, they would have. But, they have already been through a war with Israel in 2006. It would have to be a very dire situation for them to get involved in another devastating war with Israel.

As far as Fatah and the Palestinian Authority, they are essentially the same thing. The Palestinian Authority is dominated by Fatah. The Palestinian Authority came to power after the Oslo Agreement between Yasir Arafat and Bill Clinton in 1994. Under this agreement, it was decided that the Palestinian Authority would have limited powers such as policing the streets, levying taxes and basic management of the Palestinian people. It was decided that there would be no further wars between Israel and the Palestinian Authority.

Hamas refused the Oslo Agreement because Hamas believed that Israel would not respect it. They were right; Israel did not respect the agreement. This agreement stated that the West Bank belongs to the Palestinians. But now 40% of the West Bank is under Israeli settlement and occupation; and Israel wants all of the West Bank. Essentially, because Fatah and the Palestinian Authority participated in the Oslo Agreement they believe that they cannot participate in any war with Israel."

QUESTION ELEVEN

Do you think the situation would have changed if the US intervened militarily during the 11 Day Conflict? What could the US do or have done?

VOCAB

United Nations Security Council: The "primary responsibility is the maintenance of international peace and security. It has 15 Members, and each Member has one vote. Under the Charter of the United Nations, all Member States are obligated to comply with Council decisions" (un.org).

Its members: US., UK, France, China, Russia (Permanent); Estonia, India, Ireland, Kenya, Mexico, Niger, Norway, Saint Vincent and the Grenadines, Tunisia, Vietnam (Non-permanent)

"A draft resolution on non-procedural matters is adopted if nine or more of the 15 council members vote for the resolution, and if it's not vetoed by any of the five permanent members" (un.org).

RESPONSE FROM ISRAELI SOLDIER

"There was a lot of discussion among Israelis that we cannot simply solve this problem all by ourselves. We were dealing with terrorist attacks from Hamas; unfortunately, no matter how we respond we look bad in the media.

After any conflict with Gaza, Israel always sends money and humanitarian help to Gaza. But Hamas never sends anything supportive to Israel.

Also, three Israeli soldiers have been kidnapped by Hamas. They are stuck in Gaza and we can't get them out.

If any country from around the world could help, it would be greatly appreciated. It could be the US, it could be a European country, it could be the UN, it could be any country, if they could come in and somehow make sure that Hamas doesn't have any weapons, or rockets, it would be wonderful. This is because I believe that even the Gazans feel that there is too much pressure to live with Hamas but they cannot stand up against Hamas without help. Hamas has a lot of power over Gaza.

The Israelis need help. We need someone to go into Gaza and take the weapons and missiles from Hamas. But this is a very difficult decision because I know that it would be a huge sacrifice for American soldiers to come over and get involved in our conflict. I would really appreciate it if the US would help to keep the country safe in this way but we don't expect this to happen."

RESPONSE FROM CITIZEN FROM THE WEST BANK

"If the US intervened militarily it would support the Israelis. During the 11 Day Conflict the US stopped the Security Council from issuing a decision against that war four times. The US used a veto to protect Israel and to allow Israel to continue the war. We didn't expect the US to do that.

In 2014 there was a 52 Day War in Israel. The US used the veto several times to allow Israel to continue the war then as they did in the 11 Day Conflict of 2021. Personally, I think there should be international soldiers stationed between Palestine and Israel as police to protect both sides. But it should not be the US because they are biased."

QUESTION TWELVE

During the 11 Day Conflict we heard about a lot of violence in several homes and neighborhoods between Arabs and Israelis. What could have been done to prevent this?

RESPONSE FROM ISRAELI SOLDIER

"There were many acts of violence between Arabs and Israelis. We rely on intelligence to try to prevent terrorist attacks, but when someone wakes up in the morning and says 'hmmm I want to use a knife against Palestinians today' it is very difficult to prevent. Our intelligence even tries to prevent the terrorist attacks caused by the Jews against the Palestinians.

Unfortunately, there are extremists on both sides of this conflict. It is very difficult to prevent terrorist attacks that are not premeditated."

RESPONSE FROM CITIZEN FROM THE WEST BANK

"There were many unfortunate attacks on both sides; that is true. There were Israeli soldiers attacking Palestinian civilians and there were Palestinian civilians attacking Israeli civilians and soldiers. I think we have to look at the cause, the root of the problem. The media speaks about the symptoms. People didn't just wake up one morning and say 'you know what, I'm gonna launch some rockets today. I'm just gonna kill some Israelis.' It's not like that; they are fighting for something.

One example is Hamas. A lot of people label Hamas as a terrorist group. But why does Hamas exist? It was founded 30 years ago. Why? This is because of the Israeli occupation. If Palestinians felt that they had rights then there would be no reason for them to fight.

If you look historically at the Palestinian and Israeli Conflict you can see that there were some years of peace. These were the years when the Palestinians were happier. The important thing is to not look at the symptoms of a problem but the root of the problem."

QUESTION THIRTEEN

Some American media news outlets claim that Israeli soldiers should not respond with violence when they are attacked with rocks and Molotov cocktails. Do you agree?

VOCAB

Molotov Cocktail: A homemade explosive created out of a bottle and gasoline.

RESPONSE FROM ISRAELI SOLDIER

"Firstly, it depends on where you hear this in the media. If you hear it from a comedian it's based on an extreme situation. For example, there are trend videos of Arab people trying to encourage Israeli soldiers to react to their behaviors. These Israeli soldiers just stand there and do nothing in response. You have to understand that for everything the Israeli Defense force (IDF) does there is a substantial reason for that action. If we assassinate someone it is because they are planning to or have killed a Jew in a terrorist attack. We don't do anything violent without just cause.

I have been in the Navy for nine years. I am well aware of the protocol. I am not just allowed to fire at anyone for any reason."

RESPONSE FROM CITIZEN FROM THE WEST BANK

"First of all, why would a Palestinian throw a rock at an Israeli soldier? Why was there an Israeli soldier in Palestinian territory in the first place? If a Palestinian throws a rock at an Israeli soldier it's probably because they broke into the neighborhood and tried to arrest someone. You must always think about how the Palestinians feel disenfranchised. People who usually throw rocks are desperate and have no other way to express their anger. They live in suppression and misery because of the occupation."

QUESTION FOURTEEN

During the 11 Day Conflict, Netanyahu stated that he could only continue bombing or invade Gaza. Why did he make this statement?

VOCAB

Benjamin Netanyahu: He was the Caretaker Prime Minister of Israel during these interviews. He was the longest standing Prime Minister of Israel, serving for a total of 15 years.

RESPONSE FROM ISRAELI SOLDIER

"This is difficult for me to answer because I heard his speech in Hebrew, not in English, and I did not hear that statement. I do remember that he stated that if Hamas continues to shoot rockets at Israel then we will continue to bomb Hamas. If Netanyahu did make this statement, it is possible that he said it to frighten Hamas more.

Both sides try to scare each other mentally. For example, Hamas sometimes told us to get ready because at midnight we will be shooting missiles. The missiles would sometimes actually come at midnight; and other times there would be no missiles. They just want us to feel scared. They want us to stay home and not live our lives as usual. Netanyahu may have made the statement simply to keep pressure on Hamas."

RESPONSE FROM CITIZEN FROM THE WEST BANK

"Netanyahu is a very interesting Prime Minister of Israel. In fact, Israel has gone for the past 24 months without an official government because Netanyahu could not form a coalition government. He was only a caretaker Prime Minister during this conflict. He was hoping that if he won this conflict that he would become victorious in the next election for Prime Minister. This did not happen. Instead, many Israelis went out and asked him to resign." (A few weeks after our discussion Netanyahu was succeeded by Naftalie Bennett.) "Netanyahu knew that all the controversial problems that were happening in Jerusalem would lead to a war but he wanted that war so that he could stay on as Prime Minister and get more support from the people.

Netanyahu knows that when he is no longer Prime Minister he will go to prison for corruption charges because he will no longer have immunity. The war was for Netanyahu's personal political gain."

QUESTION FIFTEEN

Do you think it was necessary, and is it really true, that Israel bombarded entire neighborhoods in Gaza?

VOCAB
Human Rights Watch: "an independent, international organization that works as part of a vibrant movement to uphold human dignity and advance the cause of human rights for all" (hrw.org).

Al Jazeera News: Al Jazeera is an international news source that brings stories from around the world to people internationally in both English and Arabic. Top stories are highlighted at the top and half of every hour. It is based out of Doha, Qatar.

RESPONSE FROM ISRAELI SOLDIER
"It's not true. Israel has never destroyed an entire neighborhood, ever. We are always very specific when we target a car or an apartment. Israel did destroy the Media building that

housed Al Jazeera because Hamas intelligence operations were happening in that building below the Al Jazeera office space. That one building received very much media attention. Think about it. If one building received this much media attention we would never be able to destroy an entire neighborhood.

Also, unfortunately, Hamas is not well trained when it comes to firing rockets. Sometimes they fire rockets towards Israel but they land in their own neighborhoods in Gaza. Some Palestinians who die in Gaza die this way, being accidentally killed by Hamas. Unfortunately, there is not a lot of space in Gaza. Hamas shoots rockets from schools, playgrounds and mosques; so some of these rockets that are fired fall in Gaza and miss their targets. This is a war crime; shooting rockets from a civilian neighborhood is illegal. Sometimes Israel looks bad in the media because Israel destroys schools. But Israel would never destroy a school unless it was used as a headquarters for firing missiles and we were 100% certain that there was no one in the school."

RESPONSE FROM CITIZEN FROM THE WEST BANK

"Human Rights Watch classified the last war that Israel had with Gaza as war crime. The neighborhoods in Gaza were bombarded during the 11 Day Conflict and it was totally unnecessary to bomb entire neighborhoods in Gaza. This was both an illegal and an immoral act.

At first the Israelis were determined to smash Hamas. The Israelis didn't care about how many people were killed there. But when they destroyed the building that housed the Associated Press and Al Jazeera News, many countries started to pay attention to this conflict. The international community understood that Israel was much more advanced than Hamas and they decided to assault the media anyway. When Israel started to feel this international pressure and the intense questions from the global community regarding why Israel wanted to deter the media from being able to film and communicate to the world about the conflict, the Israelis decided that they needed to negotiate an end to this conflict."

QUESTION SIXTEEN

Do you think the conflict has ended with the cease-fire and what do you think will happen next?

RESPONSE FROM ISRAELI SOLDIER

"It has ended for now but a conflict will happen again if Hamas keeps their rockets. Unless we do something different, conflicts will keep happening.

Actually, I have an interesting anecdote for you. When I was back in Israel I met up with my friend from the Navy. We were sitting on the porch and talking about life and my sister's wedding coming up and I said 'isn't it interesting how we left the Navy a few years ago and there hasn't been a major conflict since 2014.' Whereas, prior to that, there used to be conflicts in Israel every two years. Israel had gone seven years without a major conflict. We were talking about how wonderful it was to have seven years of peace. One week later, the 11 Day Conflict ignited. Unfortunately, the conflicts will keep happening every few years.

What happens is we destroy all of Hamas' rockets and then they need time to stockpile more weapons. But if we do nothing to change the situation it will keep happening every few years."

RESPONSE FROM CITIZEN FROM THE WEST BANK

"This is the fourth war within 10 years. I think the next war will probably be worse than this 11 Day Conflict was. It will probably be more destructive and more people will die. Also,

I think the next conflict will involve the West Bank and Fatah will participate as well."

QUESTION SEVENTEEN

Do you think the cease-fire could have happened sooner?

RESPONSE FROM ISRAELI SOLDIER

"This is a difficult question to answer because when Hamas fired into Jerusalem the Israeli government soon realized that we needed to destroy a substantial amount of Hamas' rockets. We had to make sure that they realized that they cannot fire rockets into our capital city every day. We needed them to know that they can't do that every few weeks or even once a month. This was very serious to us. You could never expect to shoot missiles at the capital city of any country and anticipate zero response. For our behaviors here on earth there is payback.

I would estimate that for every day of this conflict Israel created about one month of peace. In other words, we could have resolved this conflict in one day, or in two days, but then we would enjoy only one or two months of peace. Instead we finished this conflict in 11 days. We spent 11 days destroying their missiles; I hope that this will give us at least one year of peace. In other words, the longer we attack and destroy their resources the longer the periods of peace last because they have less ammunition left to use against us."

RESPONSE FROM CITIZEN FROM THE WEST BANK

"Of course it could have happened sooner. It could've not happened at all. Hamas asked for the Israeli government to withdraw the Israeli soldiers from the Al Aqsa Mosque. It asked Israel to just let the people pray, do not provoke them, and solve the Sheik Jarrah problem. If Israel respected the

right of Muslims to pray during the holy month of Ramadan then there would have been no war. If Israel didn't send
soldiers into the Al Aqsa Mosque the war would never have
started."

QUESTION EIGHTEEN

*Both Hamas and Israel are claiming victory in the 11
Day Conflict. Who do you see as the victor?*

RESPONSE FROM ISRAELI SOLDIER

"My personal opinion is that victory connects more to a
board game. In a war you don't have a victor. Maybe Hamas
can look at it and say "we won the conflict." But I feel like both
sides lose much more than they win in every conflict.

If we finished the war with a peace agreement and we could
open the border and the Palestinians could come and work in
Israel and the Israelis could go and eat hummus and falafel in
Gaza, that for me would be a victory. But when a conflict's end
result is just quiet time, that is not a victory."

RESPONSE FROM CITIZEN FROM THE WEST BANK

"Let's go back to the analogy of the bully and the tiny guy in
the school. Who do you think won? The tiny guy who punched
the bully or the bully for pummeling the tiny guy? This is the
question.

For Palestinians, they won because they slapped the big guy
in the face. The Palestinians think that the Israelis asked for
the cease-fire. The day before the Israelis asked for the cease-
fire Netanyahu announced that they would never stop the
bombardment and that they would smash Hamas. But one day
later they caved in and asked for a cease-fire. That's why the
Palestinians see it as a victory."

QUESTION NINETEEN

What do you believe should become of Israel, the West Bank, and Gaza in the future?

RESPONSE FROM ISRAELI SOLDIER

"Oh God! I hope there will be peace! I really hope there will be peace! I hope that we can reach out to the good people in the West Bank and Gaza so that we can sit together and understand each other's pain so we can try to fix the relationship. It is possible that we can sit together and understand each other's narratives and find a solution. But we need partners.

I think that we do need a two-state solution. If we could have a one-state solution that would be wonderful; but I think the Palestinians would prefer a two-state solution."

RESPONSE FROM CITIZEN FROM THE WEST BANK

"That is very complicated. If I knew the answer, I would be a very rich guy. The first thing that needs to stop is the classification of people by the color of their skin or their religion. All Palestinians will tell you that Israelis look at us like animals. They write on the walls 'Arabs are animals.' Of course, this makes us feel sad. Sometimes we go to a school, or to a university, and we see on the walls in Hebrew statements such as 'kill Arabs' and 'Arabs are trash.' Israelis are very racist. We need to stop the racism first; then we can talk. They need to see Palestinians as normal humans. Then we can reach an agreement.

My personal opinion is that a two- state solution will never happen. The Israelis want to completely evacuate Palestine and take over everything. They want the Palestinians to disappear. It's a very sad situation but I think that there will be more wars."

QUESTION TWENTY

Is there a chance that the conflicts over Israel could escalate into a third world war?

BACKGROUND

Destruction of Temple at Temple Mount: "Biblical conspiracy theories allege the construction of a Third Holy Temple in Jerusalem will herald the end of the world. Jewish eschatology concerning the end times claims the Holy Temple will rise from the ground before the prophesied days of the apocalypse. Many Evangelists and Christian doomsday preachers believe the Third Temple will appear before the return of Jesus Christ" (keepthefaith.co.uk). Some Jewish men and women see it as a religious duty to rebuild the temple that was destroyed in 70 A.D. In order to do this, they would be required to destroy the Dome of the Rock, angering Muslims. Christians believe this will usher in the end of the world. Some Christians long for the end of the world because it means the return of Jesus Christ.

RESPONSE FROM ISRAELI SOLDIER

"Unfortunately, yes, World War III will happen if Iran and Russia react to something that angers them in support of the Palestinians. Iran is a terrorist country. They are involved in war crimes. The situation could escalate quickly because it's not just Israel. We have an agreement with countries such as the United States, the UK and Germany. If Iran and Russia escalate the situation the US, the UK and Germany will get involved and it could very well become a world war."

RESPONSE FROM CITIZEN FROM THE WEST BANK

"Unfortunately, right now there are some Jewish groups that are calling for the destruction of the Dome of the Rock and the

Al Aqsa Mosque in Jerusalem. This mosque is very important to Muslims. It is the third holiest place for 2 billion Muslim people. This has to be respected. If those groups manage to destroy the Al Aqsa Mosque I am certain that we will end up in World War III.

Not all Israelis want to destroy the mosque; but there is a small group of extremist Israelis who want to do this. Unfortunately, in the media, you don't see the normal Israelis who just live in their homes and don't want war, the same way that you don't see the normal Palestinians who just live in their homes and don't want war. Most normal people do not want war; but, the crazy people will trigger the war."

QUESTION TWENTY-ONE

What is one message you have for American students?

RESPONSE FROM ISRAELI SOLDIER

"The only message that I can offer is to really ask questions.... really ask questiaons!! Ask questions about what you see in the media. Try to look at both sides of every story you see in the media. Then, when you look at both sides, decide your opinion; but don't base it just only on one perspective. I don't want you to be pro-Israel. Also, I cannot ask you to be anti-Palestine. You can be pro-Israeli and pro-Palestinian at the same time. But you have to really make judgments about what you see, and what you hear, and try to look at facts, not opinions. Ask yourself, what is the journalist's background, because if it's someone that is an anti-Semite, then I refuse to listen to that journalist because they don't have the right to say something. Just look at the different sides of the conflict and try to look at a variety of journals, news stories, websites, and try to find the facts and then, when you have all the information and background, decide your opinion. No matter what your opinion is, I would really appreciate your opinion, if you have done research. This is the case for every conflict around the world. That is the most important message I have."

RESPONSE FROM CITIZEN FROM THE WEST BANK

"My message is don't believe the media. Don't believe Palestinians. Don't believe Israelis. Do your own research about anything. Be a critic! If on the news you see some crazy Palestinian throwing a rock towards an Israeli soldier, ask why. Why would a normal guy do that? Palestinians are people like you. They want to live. They want to enjoy their lives.

Why would a Palestinian go and join Hamas? Why would a Palestinian want to live his entire life underground, with Hamas, in the underground city they built for their protection in Gaza? Always ask why. Always understand, first, the reason why people are acting out. From there, let's build. This is because it is very easy for us to lose our mental image of conflicts between the details. Let's focus on the reasons, the root of the problem. This is my only message."

A NOTE TO TEACHERS

Have students review their answers to the graphic organizer. Ask them to discuss the following questions:

1. Do you think these two people could meet for coffee and become friends? What might they agree about? What might they argue about?
2. How could another conflict such as the 11 Day Conflict be prevented? What could the Israelis do differently? What could the Palestinians do differently?

POSSIBLE LESSON IDEA

Have students review the graphic organizer they created. Ask students which side of the conflict they empathize with more. Put them on opposite sides of the room based on the side of the conflict they empathize with. Break them into smaller groups and chunk the reading. Assign each group 3 or four of the interview questions. Have them prepare to debate the other side of the room regarding the topics in the interview questions that they are assigned.

As a possible culminating activity, visit the NaTakallam website to request an hour-long zoom experience with a refugee from the West Bank or Gaza.

The link is: https://natakallam.com/education/

Also, reach out to your local Jewish alliance foundation or a synagogue nearby and request a guest speaker from Israel, or a local rabbi, who would like to visit your classes and discuss the conflict.

Invite the guests in on separate days. Work with the students to create a list of culturally sensitive follow up questions regarding what the students are curious to learn more about.

CHAPTER SEVEN

AN INTERVIEW WITH JOANNA
FROM LEBANON

I t was one of the largest non-nuclear blasts in history. "More than 217 people were killed and 7,000 were injured when 2,750 tons of ammonium nitrate exploded in Beirut's port on 4 August 2020. The blast displaced 300,000 people and caused widespread destruction and devastation, damaging buildings up to 20km away...

Leaked official documents indicate that Lebanese customs, military, and security authorities, as well as the judiciary, had warned successive governments of the dangerous stockpile of explosive chemicals at the port on at least 10 occasions in the past six years, yet no action was taken. The president also stated that he had knowledge of the danger but had 'left it to the port authorities to address'" (Amnesty International).

The people of Lebanon have called for a thorough investigation of government officials for criminal negligence that led to the loss of 217 lives in the Beirut blast. The Lebanese officials have claimed their right to immunity throughout the investigation. However, "granting immunity to political officials directly contradicts Lebanon's obligations under the UN 2016 Minnesota protocol which aims to protect the right to life and advance justice, accountability for unlawful deaths" (Amnesty International). The government officials of Lebanon, under this protocol, were obligated to protect the lives of its citizens. As of January of 2022, the victims' families' pursuit for truth and justice regarding the blast has been obstructed.

The blast was a final straw for Lebanon. The economy had been spiraling out of control for years, and the COVID-19 pandemic, and its devastating effects on the tourism industry, were only making matters worse. The violent blast caused the Lebanese to have even less faith in their government officials and their abilities to prosper in Lebanon in the future.

Today, Lebanon's currency is steadily decreasing in value. This is causing an economic disaster. This problem started in the 1990's when Lebanon's currency was artificially propped up. The government assured that one American dollar was equal to 1500 Lebanese pounds. The problem is that Lebanon's economy was not strong enough to justify the exchange rate of 1500 Lebanese pounds to one American dollar (Al Jazeera). Thus, the value of the Lebanese currency has crashed by 90% of its value in two years. In 2022, "Lebanon kicked off the new year with the value of the pound reaching a new all-time low of 30,000 to $1.00 on the parallel market. A month earlier, it was trading at 23,000 pounds to $1.00" (Chehayeb). The result of this is that people's savings and salaries have completely bottomed out.

When Lebanon's currency became nearly worthless, it made importing goods extremely challenging. Lebanon, a small country the size of Rhode Island, imports most of its goods, especially fuel. The low value of the Lebanese pound created steep pricing for necessities such as fuel.

The Lebanese government cannot buy enough fuel for its

people. Also, it was forced to abandon some of the fuel subsidies that made fuel affordable for most people. This led to shortages and the skyrocketing of fuel prices. Everyday luxuries most people take for granted, such as getting to work or school, are becoming nearly impossible for the Lebanese.

Further, there is a shortage of fuel for generators; thus, electricity is becoming scarce. Some parts of Lebanon only have a few hours of electricity a day. This includes hospitals; in turn, the lack of fuel for generators and transportation is creating a health catastrophe.

Medicine is also imported. Similar to all other imports, medicines are becoming increasingly scarce. This includes vital medicines for diabetics and cancer patients. Every part of Lebanese society has been catastrophically impacted by the currency crisis. Ultimately, Lebanon has become a country with few government services.

The cause of the economic destruction points to the creation of the Lebanese government. Following WWI, the League of Nations mandated that Lebanon be controlled by France. "The first Lebanese constitution was drafted in 1926" (carnegieendowment.org). It was specifically designed by France to share power among the three main religious sects. "The president must always be Maronite Christian, the Prime Minister a Sunni and the speaker of Parliament a Shia" (euronews. com). In 1932, the French designed the Lebanese government to give more power to the Maronite Christians. The Christian president was given veto power over all legislation. Also, the parliament seats were established as six Christian members compared to only five Muslim members. Unfortunately, this led to gridlock and infighting as each religious sect attempted to gain power and favor for its own people.

In 2019, the Lebanese people started calling for a social revolution "against the political elite" (Al Jazeera). By August of

2020, the situation only became worse when a horrific explosion rocked the Beirut port. No one has been held accountable for this disaster. Many people blame the Lebanese government for malfeasance.

JOANNA'S STORY

Joanna is a charismatic 37-year-old woman from Lebanon. She has a nine-year-old son. She has thick, curly hair and a bit of French in her Lebanese accent, probably due to the French colonization of Lebanon from 1920 "until it achieved its independence in 1943" (Britannica.com). She remembers her youth fondly. She loved growing up in the small village of Hemlaya. She and her friends played outside together from dawn until dusk. She continues to love how her village is very close knit. Everyone knows each other and supports each other as best they can.

Her nine-year-old son enjoys spending his time on his iPad, watching videos on YouTube, or playing games. She prefers watching her son play the drums or the derbaki, a small Middle Eastern style drum, also known as a goblet drum, pictured below. He has been taking derbaki lessons for five years.

However, the economic crisis has been extremely hard on her and everyone around her. She wishes that she could move to another country with a better economy where she could work for a better future for herself and her son. Unfortunately, she is not able to move out of the country.

Additionally, she experiences other economic hardships. First of all, in Lebanon, it is frowned upon for a woman to get divorced. To compound this, when Lebanese women get divorced they are not entitled to their husband's income following the divorce. In Joanna's case, she needed to move in with her parents for financial support and pursue a new career,

as she was a stay at home mother when she was married. She really appreciates that she had the support of her parents during her divorce and now. Without them, her situation may have been as dire as many other women who have no choice but to stay in unhappy marriages for financial reasons.

I interviewed Joanna on February 17, 2022. We met via

zoom. She was in Lebanon; I was in the United States.

PART ONE

VOCAB

Economy: "The wealth and resources of a country or region, especially in terms of the production and consumption of goods and services" (Oxford Languages).

Economic Crisis: "A situation in which the economy of a country experiences a sudden downturn in its aggregate output or real gross domestic product (GDP)" (igidashglobal.com).

Revolution: "A forcible overthrow of a government or social order, in favor of a new system" (Oxford Languages).

Pound: The Lebanese pound is the Lebanese currency.

GUIDING QUESTION

Why is it important for a government to provide its citizens with basic needs?

"How has the economic crisis affected you and your friends and family in Lebanon?" I asked.

"The economy has suffered greatly since the revolution of 2019. Everyone has been affected by it. The Lebanese pound is worth 0.00066% of the American dollar and its value keeps dropping. Yet, the Lebanese people continue to be paid in this worthless currency. It creates a situation where working has almost no value. It is almost impossible for Lebanese people to live the way we were living two years ago. The cost of food and fuel to drive to work, or to transport children to school, has become astronomical.

A few years ago Lebanese people who were employed were able to go out to eat, or go to a café and buy coffee, regularly. Now, almost no one can afford to eat well every day. I noticed that some of my friends who used to eat at restaurants regularly sacrifice decent meals for as much as three days in a row, just to afford to order a cup of coffee or a slice of cake at a cafe. Almost no one has any surplus money to have fun or to travel anymore.

The cost of living has risen sharply; but, my salary has decreased more than three times what it was two years ago. Further, many Lebanese merchants such as pharmacies, insurance carriers and auto mechanics only accept payment in American dollars. This makes it even more challenging to pay for what we need. This is because the Lebanese pound that we are paid in continues to drop in value each day.

Last year my medical insurance was 800 American dollars at the rate of 1,500 Lebanese pounds per US dollar. This means that I paid about 1,200,000 Lebanese pounds for my $800.00 medical insurance. Now my insurance is 500 American dollars but at the daily rate of the pound, which changes each day. Right now it's 33,000 pounds for each American dollar. In other words my insurance is now 16,500,000 Lebanese pounds per year. Essentially, my yearly medical insurance bill is 16 times as expensive as it was one year ago. It is actually twice my monthly salary, and prices are continuing to rise. I could only afford to pay 25% of it. The insurance carrier offered me a payment plan. I am to pay 25% of it this month and divide the rest of the money I owe into other payments for nine months. In other words, the insurance carrier offered me nine months to make good on the payments I owe. This is why there is no money left for Lebanese people to have fun and do leisure activities. They are struggling to pay for their basic needs.

The economic crisis has affected the hospitals and the availability of healthcare. It is difficult for Lebanon to import the medicines we need because our currency's value is so low. Sometimes I need to return to the doctor several times to see if the doctor has received the medications I need from the few shipments of goods that do make their way into Lebanon.

Recently my son had an ear infection. I called his doctor and he told me to buy him Otipax; but it was not available. So I called his doctor again and I had no choice but to buy him Augmentin, even though my son had no fever and Augmentin is usually for fevers. It was terrifying and heartbreaking to be unable to help my child, who was in so much pain, because there was no medication for him.

The other problem is the high price of gasoline; it is about ten times as expensive as it was a year ago. I can barely afford to drive myself to work. When my son stays with his father he can take the school bus. However, when he stays with me, here at my parents' home, I need to drive him to school because he cannot be registered for two different buses at the same time.

Furthermore, electricity is incredibly expensive and it works for a maximum of about two hours per day. To compound this, we never know when we will get our two hours of electricity. My parents and I split the cost of it, 1 million pounds per month. Sometimes the electricity only works for 50 minutes per day.

We also pay to use our village generator. This service is approximately 4,000,000 Lebanese pounds each month. Also, remember, generators run on fuel, which is highly expensive, so we need to minimize the generator's use as much as possible. I prioritize two chores when the power is on, ironing and washing clothes in the washing machine. Sometimes the electricity turns off and my clothes don't finish. Other times the power will be out for as long as two days and the clothes will be wet and stuck in the washing machine for days. Right now I have no electricity. I can talk to you via zoom because the generator is on. During the evenings, once the sun sets, the streets of Lebanon are completely black. It is a sad sight to see because it used to be a country that was bubbling with excitement and lights.

GUIDING QUESTION

Why is it important for a government to provide its citizens with basic needs?

PART TWO

VOCAB

Ammonium Nitrate: "A white crystalline solid used as a fertilizer and as a component of some explosives" (Oxford Languages).

GUIDING QUESTION

Why is it important for government officials to be held accountable for their actions?

"Joanna, can you speak a bit about the explosion in the port of Beirut this summer?" I asked.

"First of all, we still do not know what really happened regarding the explosion. We do not know why hundreds of tons of ammonium nitrate were stored in a rundown warehouse at the port of Beirut for six years. This is equivalent to 1,200 tons of TNT and it caused an earthquake strength blast. 217 people died, 7,000 people were wounded and 300,000 people lost their homes and businesses. Half of our capital city was damaged.

I was far away from Beirut when the explosion happened, enjoying a summer day at the beautiful beach in Amchit. This beach is about a 45-minute drive from Beirut; but I heard the explosion twice. No one understood what happened and everyone was trying to get home for their safety. There was a tremendous amount of traffic and many streets were completely closed off. It took me hours to get home.

The situation was sad and terrifying. That day gravely affected every Lebanese person. Innocent people lost their lives for no reason. As a mother, what bothers me the most is that mothers lost their children. To me, there is nothing worse than the loss of a child.

There are several theories still circulating regarding what happened. I reviewed many videos of the explosion that were posted on Facebook, Instagram, and the local news here.

The widely accepted truth is that Lebanese security and government officials knew that ammonium nitrate was being haphazardly stored in this warehouse; but nothing was done about it. The Lebanese people are calling for the government to be held accountable for what happened in the port of Beirut that day; but amazingly no one has been held accountable yet. There has been an investigation here in Lebanon. Unfortunately, there has been much corruption, political interference, and many problems with due process. Thus, the case is not nearly resolved.

It seems that no one cares about Lebanon. The international community really must step in and do an independent investigation of what went wrong and why these people died."

GUIDING QUESTION

Why is it important for government officials to be held accountable for their actions?

PART THREE

GUIDING QUESTION

Is a desperate situation a justification for making an unethical decision?

"Have the people of Lebanon noticed the assistance from the UN, the NGOs, or the international community?" I asked.

"The UN and the NGOs have sent medicine and food to us. I have a cousin who is living in Cyprus. She assisted the NGOs who were supplying the Lebanese people with goods from Cyprus. Further, Saudi Arabia, Qatar, Bahrain, India and many other countries also helped us.

Unfortunately, many of the supplies that were sent by the NGOs to be given away for free to the Lebanese people were stolen and sold for profit. Some of the supplies were even sold in other countries. Other items were sold here in Lebanese markets. These items were supposed to be given away for free because they were humanitarian aid; but instead they were sold by desperate people who needed money. We know this was happening because the products were labeled in Arabic and in English as donations; but they still had price tags on them, and vendors were expecting to be paid for these items. This includes food items such as cheese but it also includes medicine as well. Even PCR tests to test for COVID-19 were donated but sold for profit by the locals here. Lebanon is very corrupt.

There are other people who have made terrible decisions because of their desperate situations. For example, I hear often on the news that burglaries have happened at pharmacies and markets. There are also home break-ins fairly regularly. Just today I heard on the news that in a village to the north of Lebanon there was a home invasion. The burglars assaulted the woman who was home alone and they stole six million pounds from her. This may sound like a lot of money; but it's actually only 200 American dollars. I worry that crime will happen more frequently if the economic situation continues to deteriorate further.

GUIDING QUESTION

> *Judge the decisions of the Lebanese people who committed crimes and sold donated supplies. Does their economic situation justify their decisions?*

PART FOUR

GUIDING QUESTION

Why are free government elections important?

" I heard that Lebanon has a new government as of January of 2022. This new government is projecting itself as a government that is for the people. Is this the case?", I asked.

"The only change that is actually happening in our life is that goods are getting more and more expensive. Nothing has improved. Food, fuel, Internet and electricity are only more expensive. There is no progress. The same corruption that happened here years ago is continuing. The protests are dying down and the suffering is continuing.

We all endure the daily stress of the economy. There is not much that the Lebanese people can do. Besides, people have been protesting for two years and they never got anything out of it. We hope for a new and better Lebanon; but most of our young people are immigrating to other countries. People are selling their homes to build new lives in other countries and it is creating a brain drain for Lebanon. The best and brightest people, the ones who have the skills to become doctors and politicians, are leaving our country behind.

New government elections are happening in May of 2022. We hope for a new and better Lebanon. But it is unlikely because our elections are always corrupt. I have heard that politicians often pay Lebanese citizens for their votes. People are paid anywhere from $100 to $200, possibly more, for their votes. Even though we do have secret ballots here in Lebanon, if someone is paid to vote for a certain politician they will do so. We understand the level of corruption here. The politicians know exactly how many votes they paid for and compare it to the number of votes that they received. Lebanese people are too afraid to accept bribe money for a vote and not actually vote that way. But they also need to agree to take the bribe money because they are desperate for money. Thus, because the elections are literally purchased by the politicians, nothing changes. The people need the money, so they accept the bribes, and they vote in the same politicians that have created the corruption. This causes a vicious cycle and nothing changes here in Lebanon.

We need a new government. Lebanon is dying. But we still have hope. My big dream is to own my own home where I can live with my son. But with the economic crisis now I can't live on my own without the financial support of my parents. At this point, it is difficult for me to admit this, but I have given up on this dream, for now. Maybe it will happen in the future.

What is one final message that you have for American students?

"Come and visit Lebanon. Get to know our families and our traditions. We would be happy to have you visit here. Get to know us as people. You will love visiting with us! We have a beautiful country."

GUIDING QUESTION

What are the consequences of the corruption during Lebanese government elections?

PRINTABLE WORKSHEET FOR TEACHERS

Guiding Question	Answer before reading the section	Answer after reading the section
Part 1: Why is it important for a government to provide its citizens with basic needs?		
Part 2: Why is it important for government officials to be held accountable for their actions?		
Part 3: Is a desperate situation a justification for making an unethical decision?		
Part 4: Why are free government elections important?		

As a possible culminating activity, visit the NaTakallam website to request an hour-long zoom experience with a refugee from Lebanon. You may be assigned Joanna herself! Make sure to inform NaTakallam that you read this chapter from *Refugee Realities.*

This is the link: https://natakallam.com/education/

ACKNOWLEDGEMENTS

A book such as this is impossible without the generosity of many people. Foremost among them are the nine people whose stories I tell. I offer my deepest gratitude to Malika, Mohammad, Layla, Rahim, Balsam, Salam, Orit, Salman, and Joanna.

I am deeply indebted to the Qatar Foundation for awarding me a grant for funding and to work with NaTakallam on retaining many of the interviews for this book.

Refugee Realities would also be impossible without the tireless efforts of everyone at NaTakallam. Two employees there, in particular, have made this book possible, Madison Sindorf and Carmela Francolino. Madison supported me and set up several of my interviews. She is also assisting me with advertising. Carmela also supported me in helping to distribute this book across the country.

If you are interested in hosting a conversation with a refugee, or taking a language lesson from a refugee through NaTakallam, the purchase of this book comes with a 15% off coupon code- (STORIES15). Simply apply this code at checkout. Teachers are more than welcome to share this code with their students as well.

Please email academics@mail-natakallam.com with subject line *"Refugee Realities"* and NaTakallam's Academic Programs Director can provide additional information, as well as a discounted price quote.

Finally, my greatest debt is to Gerald Schiano, my father, who spoke with me often about my passion for understanding refugees and introducing students to their stories. He acted as my first audience and inspired me to keep going with my pursuit to share refugee stories with other educators and students around the world. His energy and passion are immeasurable.

REFERENCES

CHAPTER ONE

Introduction

"For 48 hours, 30,000 families (https://www.wbur.org) (Dec 2021).

"ISIS Tricked A Mother Into Eating Her Own Son" By Sadho Ram — 01 Jul 2017, 01:44 PM <https://says.com/my/news/an-iraqi-lawmaker-claims-isis-tricked-a-mother-into-eating-her-own-son> (Dec 2021).

Part 1

"A person regarded as an inspired teacher or proclaimer of the will of God." (Oxford languages).

"An endorsement on a passport..." (resources.evoyglobal.com).

Part 2

"Persuasive mass communication that filters and frames the issues of the day..." (oxfordreference.com).

"A group of people whose practices, race, religion, ethnicity, or other characteristics..." (Wikipedia).

Part 3

"Specific crimes committed in the control of a large-scale attack targeting civilians..." (trialinternational.org).

"A nonprofit organization that operates independently of any government..." (Oxford languages).

Part 4

"An action that is taken or an order that is given, to force a country to obey international laws..." (Merriam-Webster.com).

Part 5
"A militant Kurdish nationalist organization..." (Britannica)

CHAPTER 2

Part 1
"In the era of Saddam Hussein, Abu Ghraib": The New Yorker, April 30, 2004.
"Shia: One of the two main branches of Islam, followed especially in Iran":
   Oxford Dictionary
"Sunni: The larger of the two main branches of Islam": Oxford Dictionary
"Was allowed to assist the Prophet in cleansing": Reza Aslan, No god but God
   The Origins, Evolution, and Future of Islam (New York: Random House
   Trade Paperbacks, 2011), 118.
"The Yezidis is one of many religious minorities in Iraq. They follow Yezidism":
   Norwegian Refugee Council <https://www.nrc.no/news/2018/december/
   five-things-you-should-know-about-the-yazidis/#:~:text=The%20Yezidis%20
   is%20one%20of,the%20Earth%20in%20God's%20place.>.
"A major religion stemming from the life, teachings and death of Jesus of
   Nazareth.": Britiannica.com
"President of Iraq from 1979-2003 when he was hanged by the American
   coalition forces": Britannica.com
"Saddam Hussein's political party. It was known for totalitarianism and
   brutality": pbs.org
ISIS: The Islamic State of Iraq and Syria: Britannica.com
"Nouri al-Maliki became the deputy leader of the Supreme National Debaathi-
   fication Commission": DW.com

Part 2
"Deradicalization: The process of encouraging a person with extreme political,
   social or religious views to adopt a more moderate approach.": wikipedia.com

Part 3
"Legal prohibition by a government or group of governments resisting the
   departure of vessels or movement of goods from some or all locations to
   one or more countries.": Britannica.com
"Actual or threatened punishments: for example refusing to export, refusing to

import, refusing to trade.": Britannica.com

"Britain blocked Iraq's access to the Persian Gulf by severing the territorial entity, 'Kuwait' from the rest of Iraq in 1921" (Mechanisms of Western Domination: A Short History of Iraq and Kuwait by David Klein)

"Drilling $2.4 billion worth of Iraqi oil at the border.": Whose Wars? Teaching about the Iraq War and the War on Terrorism (Milwaukee: Rethinking Schools, Ltd., 2005), 17.

"Totalitarian: Form of government that prohibits individual freedom": Britannica.com

This monster later befriends a young girl in the nearby countryside but then inadvertently drowns her": Britannica.com

"Half a million children died as a result of the sanctions": Reuters, July, 21. 2000.

Part 4

"A condition that exists when someone has lost control of something, and no one has replaced them.": Cambridge Dictionary

"Sovereignty: The authority of a state to govern itself.": Britannica.com

Part 5

AAH: Asaib Ahl al-Haqor AKA League of Righteous- Shia militant group. It wants Iraq to be a "Shia controlled state." It also wants "to expel the remaining US military and diplomatic presence from the country.": understandingthwar.org

"Kidnapped British computer consultant Peter Moore to exchange with Iraqi prisoners taken by Britain": the Guardian

Part 9

"On June 23, 2009, a spontaneous mass demonstration erupted in Iran": Al Jazeera, June 12, 2013

Part 10

Qasem Soleimani: "An Iranian major general and commander of the Qudz force, a wing of the Islamic Revolutionary Guard Corps responsible for foreign operations.": (Britannica)

"Knew were committed to guarding Iran's new political system and the ideals of the Islamic revolution.": (Washington Post, Jan 4, 2020)

CHAPTER 3

Introduction

"Canceled as five people were reportedly killed at the airport as people scrambled to leave Afghanistan" Deaths, gunshots reported at Kabul airport as
  chaos continues 16 August 2021 (Al Jazeera).

"Handed in desperation to a soldier across an airport wall" Afghan Baby
  Lost in Kabul Airlift Chaos Reunited with Relatives 10 January 2022 (Al
  Jazeera).

One individual who died this way was Zaki Anwari, a 17-year-old member of
  Afghanistan's national youth soccer team "A 17-year-old Afghan youth
  soccer player died falling from a US evacuation plane" by Farnaz Fassihi
  (August 19, 2021) the New York Times.

A second person was Fada Mohammed, a young dentist " The story of an
  Afghan man who fell from the sky" By Gerry Shih, Niha Masih, Dan
  Lamoth (August, 16, 2021) The Washington Post

Part 1

"Ultraconservative political and religious faction..." (Britannica) (Feb 2022).

Background

"2,996 people died..." (September 11th - 102 Minutes That Shocked
  the World - Part 3" documentary, <https://www.youtube.com/
  watch?v=P28YCK68wGc>.

"Researchers have identified more than 60 types of cancer..." Scientific America
  Health Effects of 9/11 Still Plague Responders and Survivors, Tara Haelle,
  10 September 2021.

"The people who knocked these buildings down will hear all of us soon" (fox29.
  com).

"We will never forget" (WCTV.tv) Published: Sep. 11, 2022 at 10:34 AM
  EDT|Updated: Sep. 11, 2022 at 5:38 PM EDT (Feb 2022).

"On October 7, 2001, a U.S. led coalition..." (history.com) (Feb 2022).

"THE HUMAN COST" Cost of the Afghanistan War in Lives and Dollars:
  Ellen Nickmeyer, 17 August 2021 Associated Press

CHAPTER 4

The Home That Was Our Country: A Memoir of Syria by Malek (Nation Books;
  1st Edition., 2017), 167.

The Daughters of Kobani: A Story of Rebellion, Courage, and Justice by

Lemmon (Penguin Books; 2021), 33,34.

Part 1
"The Arab Spring was a movement..." (Kids Britannica).

Part 2
"A follower of 'Ali,' the Prophet..." (Encyclopedia.com).
"The geographic region located between the Mediterranean Sea" (history.com).
"The Salafi-jihadi ideology, which has existed" (criticalthreats.org).
"A Sunni Salafist militant group operating in Syria" (stanford.edu).
"An Islamic fundamentalist who participates in, or supports, jihad" (dictionary.
   com).

Part 4
"A writ requiring a person under arrest to be brought before a judge or into
   court" (Oxford Languages).

Part 5
"One of the indigenous people of the Mesopotamia..." (voanews.com) (Feb
   2021).

CHAPTER 5

Introduction
"In ancient times Yemen was known as Arabia Felix..." (The Guardian).
According to UNICEF, Yemen is the world's largest humanitarian crisis...
   (UNICEF.org).
"Dancing on the heads of snakes" Newsmaker: Yemen's Saleh, "dancing on
   the heads of snakes" Reuters Staff <https://www.reuters.com/article/
   us-yemen-saleh/newsmaker-yemens-saleh-dancing-on-the-heads-of-snakes-
   idUSTRE78M20X20110923>.
"32bn and $60bn during 33 years in power" (Al Jazeera). UN says ex-Yemen
   president Saleh stole up to $60bn 25 Feb 2015 <https://www.aljazeera.
   com/news/2015/2/25/un-says-ex-yemen-president-saleh-stole-up-to-60bn>.
"The protesters began to call upon President Ali Abdullah Saleh to
   resign......" (Oxford Constitutional Law) <https://oxcon.ouplaw.com/
   search?ct=9a0420dd-e6df-491d-aec8-4d0a6c78f11a> (Feb 2021).
"the Saudi led coalition has conducted more than 20,100 airstrikes on
   Yemen...." Roth, Kenneth. "World Report 2020: Yemen." Human Rights

Watch, <https://www.hrw.org/world-report/2020/country-chapters/yemen>
(Feb 2021).

"Since 2015, 18,000 Yemeni civilians have been killed or wounded...." UN:
18000 Yemeni airstrike casualties since 2015." AP News, 9 September 2021,
<https://apnews.com/article/middle-east-united-nations-yemen-houthis-bd-
e67c6d3f0c3007410134e9f2963ad3> (Feb 2021).

"Houthi strike in Saudi Arabia...." (CNBC) PUBLISHED WED, SEP 18
2019 10:53 AM EDT UPDATED WED, SEP 18 2019 3:08 PM EDT
<https://www.cnbc.com/2019/09/18/saudi-arabia-drone-and-missile-debris-
proves-iranian-role-in-attack.html> (Feb 2021).

"'We're ending all American support for offensive operations in the war in
Yemen...." <https://www.theguardian.com/world/2021/feb/04/us-end-sup-
port-saudi-led-operations-yemen-humanitarian-crisis> (Feb 2021).

"Seized new territory in the energy-rich provinces of Shabwa and Marib....."
"Many killed in Houthi missile attack on mosque, says minister." Al Jazeera,
1 November 2021, https://www.aljazeera.com/news/2021/11/1/houthi-mis-
sile-attack-on-mosque-kills-29-says-yemen-minister> (Feb 2021).

Part 1
"A person who has been forced to leave their country in order to escape war...."
(Oxford Languages).

Part 6
"An action that is taken or an order that is given to force a country to obey
international laws...." (Merriam-Webster.com).

Part 8
"A system, weapon, or technology involved in the detection, tracking, interception, and destruction of attacking missiles" (Wikipedia).

Part 9
"On July 14, 2015 the P5+1...." "Joint Comprehensive Plan of Action." 2009—
2017 State.gov, <https://2009-2017.state.gov/e/eb/tfs/spi/iran/jcpoa/index.
htm. Accessed 30 October 2022> (Feb 2021).
"Eliminate" <https://www.jcpa.org/jl/vp536.htm>.

Part 10
"A proxy war occurs when a major power instigates or plays a major role in
supporting..." (brookings.edu).

Part 11

"The countries of the world considered collectively" (Oxford Languages).

"A relationship between two countries in which they send diplomats..." (macmillandictionary.com).

"A group of people with similar political goals and opinions. The purpose is to get candidates elected to public office" (yourdictionary.com).

CHAPTER 6

Introduction

586 B.C. when the Babylonian Empire conquered the Israelites, and the Ark, at the time, supposedly stored in the temple of Jerusalem, vanished from history" (national geographic).

"The place where creation began, and the site where Abraham was poised to sacrifice Isaac" (smithsonianmag.com).

"Why Jerusalem is not the capital of Israel." Al Jazeera, 10 December 2017, <https://www.aljazeera.com/features/2017/12/10/why-jerusalem-is-not-the-capital-of-israel> (October 2022).

"Israel passed the 'Jerusalem law'" Nashashibi, Sharif. "Why Jerusalem is not the capital of Israel." Al Jazeera, 10 December 2017, <https://www.aljazeera.com/features/2017/12/10/why-jerusalem-is-not-the-capital-of-israel> (October 2022).

"Judaism's holiest place of prayer. The West Wall is part of the Temple Mount's retaining wall, built by Herod the Great in the first century B.C. (Top 10 Israel and Petra by Eyewitness Travel).

"253 Palestinians were killed..." <https://www.aljazeera.com/news/2021/5/30/waking-up-screaming-gazan-children-traumatised-by-israeli-war>. By Maram Humaid. Published On 30 May 2021. Updated: 1 Jun 202108:09 AM (GMT) (Al Jazeera).

"The Arab World consists of 22 countries in the Middle East" (middleeastpdx.org).

"A native or inhabitant of the Republic of Israel" (webster.com).

"Belonging or relating to the region..." (collinsdictionary.com).

"Hamas: The Palestinian militant group that rules Gaza." BBC, 1 July 2021, <https://www.bbc.com/news/world-middle-east-13331522> (October 2022).

Question 3

"The events of 1948 when many Palestinians were displaced..." (Oxford

Languages).

Question 5
"Rural Communities Salute Jerusalem...." (main.knesset.gov).

Question 11
"Primary responsibility is the maintenance of international peace and secu-
rity...." (un.org).
"A draft resolution on non-procedural matters..." (un.org).

Question 16
"An independent, international organization that works as part of a vibrant
movement to uphold human dignity and advance the cause of human
rights for all" (hrw.org).

Question 21
"Biblical conspiracy theories allege..." (keepthefaith.co.uk)

CHAPTER 7

Introduction
"More than 217 people were killed and 7,000 were injured...(Amnesty
International) <https://www.amnesty.org/en/latest/news/2021/08/leba-
non-one-year-on-from-beirut-explosion-authorities-shamelessly-obstruct-jus-
tice/> (Feb 2021).
"Granting immunity to political officials....." (Amnesty International) <https://
www.amnesty.org/en/latest/news/2021/08/lebanon-one-year-on-from-bei-
rut-explosion-authorities-shamelessly-obstruct-justice/> (Feb 2021).
"Not strong enough to justify the exchange rate of 1500 Lebanese pounds
to one American dollar" Chehayeb, Kareem. "Value of Lebanese pound
drops to all-time low." Al Jazeera, 26 May 2022, <https://www.aljazeera.
com/news/2022/5/26/lebanese-pound-value-drops-to-lowest-level> (October
2022).
"Lebanon kicked off the new year with the value of the pound reaching a new
all-time low of 30,000 to $1.00 on the parallel market." Al Jazeera news:
Lebanon's crippled economy hobbles into New Year" by Kareem Chehayeb.
"The first Lebanese constitution was drafted in 1926" (carnegieendowment.
org).
"The president must always be Maronite Christian, the Prime Minister a Sunni

and the speaker of Parliament a Shia" (euronews.com).

In 2019, the Lebanese people started calling for a social revolution "against the political elite" (Al Jazeera).

Until it achieved its independence in 1943" (Britannica.com).

Part 1

"The wealth and resources of a country or region, especially in terms of the production and consumption of goods and services" (Oxford Languages).

"A situation in which the economy of a country experiences a sudden downturn in its aggregate output or real gross domestic product (GDP)" (igidashglobal.com).

"A forcible overthrow of a government or social order, in favor of a new system" (Oxford Languages).

Part 2

"A white crystalline solid used as a fertilizer and as a component of some explosives" (Oxford Languages).

Part 3

"An international organization that aims to increase political and economic cooperation..." (Investopedia).

"A nonprofit organization that operates independently........" (Oxford languages)

"The countries of the world considered collectively"" (Oxford Languages).

ABOUT THE AUTHOR

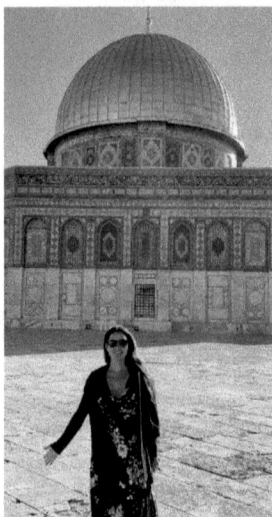

Tara Seger, M.S. has spent 16 years researching the Middle East. Her focus has been on conflict zones and refugees. Her research includes traveling to the United Arab Emirates with the World Affairs Council. She also studied extensively at Yad Vashem, the world renowned Holocaust Museum in Jerusalem, Israel. She completed additional research in the West Bank, Nazareth, Tiberius, Caesarea, and Tel Aviv. Tara Seger has personally interviewed dozens of refugees from conflict zones in the Middle East. She is a veteran teacher of Middle East Conflicts, Modern World History, US History II, and US History II Honors at Scituate High School in North Scituate, Rhode Island, USA. She was invited to speak at the SOCIO-INT International Conference on Education and Humanities Conference in Istanbul, Turkey regarding the unique curriculum she developed for her students. Tara Seger has successfully merged her master's degree training in curriculum design with her B.A. in History. She combined her unique lesson design with her extensive research of the Middle East to create a book that is easily accessible to young minds while inspiring adults and teens to objectively analyze the causes and consequences of Middle Eastern conflicts.